AF244647

HARD HEAD
CITY

CALVIN KERR, JR.

CONTENTS

From the Author

Throughout my military and civilian careers, I have had the opportunities to work in many diverse occupations and positions. Some of the jobs include: First Sergeant, Army Instructor (Junior Reserve Officer Training Corps), High School Basketball Coach, Registered Dental Hygienist, Real Estate Consultant, Financial Advisor with securities 6 and 63 certifications, Drill Instructor, Calvary Scout, Infantryman, Track Commander, Machine Gunner, Grenadier, and Rifleman. Sometimes, the aforementioned jobs entailed being placed in many unpleasant places. The Demilitarized Zone in Korea and the Jungles of Panama are two places that come to mind. However, I must admit that one of my biggest disappointments occurred when I was released by an Air Force Colonel at the Pentagon and found myself without a job. I never imagined that after at least forty years of service (22 active) with the Army, I did not even rate an interview. Although I felt empty at the time without a job, it turned out to be a blessing because it allotted me the time to finish this book. However, I do make the sacrifice of being away from my family to have a job. Moreover, working out of another state away from home is utmost difficult. My resolve is that I do have a job to support my family.

The experience of working in the aforementioned occupations and positions allowed me to gain camaraderie with many people and become familiar with numerous places in United States and abroad. It is through my acquaintance with those people and places that I ascertained knowledge to write my short stories.

Anyway, I thank God for the ability and skills to write this book. The events that took place in this book are all based on true stories. The short stories you are about to engage in were witnessed by me (the author) or told to me by the storyteller. In most cases, names, as well as locations, have been changed to protect the identity and rights of people actually involved.

City Of Flames And Falling Stars

A Prelude To Black Mondays

She sparkles and glows atop
the Mississippi River banks,
with the developing states
of Arkansas and Mississippi to her flanks.

She hosts the world famous Beale Street,
where prostitutes used to…
and jazz and blues singers still meet.

Her people show much interest,
in fancy clothes and "Cadillac Cars."
I often to refer to her
as the "City of Flames and Fallen Stars."

Great people have come from this city,
including "Elvis" and his band.
In fact one of her famous landmarks
is the "King's Graceland."
Martin marched on her city hall,
in the spring of sixty eight.
He led a protest for sanitation workers.
Violence and bloodshed ignited with his fate.

Her people show much interest,
in fancy clothes and "Cadillac Cars."
I often refer to her
as the "City of Flames and Fallen Stars."

She is renowned for "Stax Records,"
where many artists got their start.
Yes, the sweet soul songs,
are still near and dear to my heart.

I remember the firemen strike.
It was like déjà vu,
I do believe.

The many fires caused a ten o'clock Curfew.
I never forgot the burning she would receive.

Her people show much interest,
in fancy clothes and "Cadillac Cars."
I often refer to her
as the "City of Flames and Fallen Stars."

She has made much progress,
but more face lifts are due.
She sports places like the "Pyramid" And "Mud Island."
She has elected a black mayor, too.
In May she sparkles, and in July she glows.
She is very entertaining to watch, with her "Goodwill Shows."

Her people show much interest,
in fancy clothes and "Cadillac Cars."
I often to refer to her
as the "City of Flames and Fallen Stars."

She could use more unity,
from her black and white girls and boys.
'though at times so peaceful,
and other times, she is a battlefield for "Star Wars."

Her people show much interest,
in fancy clothes and "Cadillac Cars."
I often refer to her
as the "City of Flames and Fallen Stars."

Black Mondays

WOKE UP TO SMELL THE COFFEE

As I entered the small building that is set apart from Mitchell Road High School's main facility, my tall scrawny body in dripping, soaked clothes shivered from the cold-chilling weather. My body had been helpless against the bludgeoning globs of raindrops. I felt stoned during the the two-plus-mile walk to get to school. My blue-and-pink alpaca sweater, blue cotton jacket, and blue jeans were no match for this sort of weather. To add insult to injury, my grandfather's old shoes were a little too big. They were miserably awkward and just downright embarrassing. Soaked from head to toe, immediately, I sought the furnace alongside the wall of the classroom. That uncomfortable moment is one reflection of events I experienced in getting to school.

Sometimes the other kids and I took a shortcut, trespassing through people's yards. The shortcut took us through the path by a scary looking house we referred to as the "Adams Family House." It was a big, seemingly abandoned house that one would imagine seeing in a horror movie. Ghost tales added to its mystic, and I must admit an eerie feeling came over every time I walked by that place.

We lived in a part of the school district not funded for buses (the new sub). Mainly, students at Mitchell Road High School were categorized into four groups based on their residency. The groups were informally referred to as the new sub, the old sub, the junction, and box-town. Our neighborhood consisted of small, single family homes. We were one of the first families to move into the newly developed neighborhood, the new sub or Walker Homes. The old sub was more north of Mitchell Road and for the most part ended east of Ford Road. The junction began just west of Ford road and ended at the railroad tracks. Box-town set southwest across the railroad tracks. Because we lived in the new sub, we were misperceived as being well-to-do. Little did our schoolmates know that we ate the same government cheese, bologna and peanut that they did. Honestly, we probably struggled more than any family, new sub, old sub, junction, or box-town.

Although desegregation was attempted to equalize the unfair distribution of school funds and other like items, it was not easily accepted. Literally, the city tried to force the issue. I experienced the reluctance first hand. It was not hard to determine that Mitchell Road High School never had more than five Caucasians enrolled at any one time. Usually, they were placed in special education programs. At any given school year, there were more white teachers than white students.

During the sixties, Memphis was like an active volcano fueled by racial injustices. It was a mid-south town vastly torn by a dividing line between its black and white populations. Moreover, the "good ole boy" system was in full effect.

In other words, racial equality was a volatile issue. Not only was it volatile in Memphis but it also affected mainstream America as well. Discrimination and prejudice were so obvious that a blind man could see it. It showed its ugly face in many areas: workplaces, educational institutions, military branches, law enforcement agencies, social venues, and many other arenas. Vindictive white people in small southern towns made no doubt about where they stood. The evidence usually smacked one dead in the face. Indicatively, signs such as For Whites Only were seen on restroom doors.

The sign was one of the lashes that slapped me out of the dumb daze in thinking that all was equal. I saw my first one on a road trip with my father when I had to use the bathroom. We stopped at a rural town between Memphis and St. Louis. When we stopped, my father immediately noticed and pointed to the writing outside the toilet. Prior to that moment, I had never sensed fear from him. I did not think that he was afraid of anything. I suppose at the time I was too young to notice many subtle hints of racism. I had not been exposed to the indecent and inhumane treatment of blacks, so I did not understand the mentality of some white people. Finally, I woke up to "smell the coffee." I realized that we were forbidden to eat in the same establishments as whites. Now, my rule of thumb is, if you are not welcome, do not go.

Back then, blacks were more often found behind the scenes. In most restaurants and kitchens, they were the cooks and the dishwashers. Occasionally, a waitress or busboy would be seen in the eating area. However, other labor jobs were available: sanitation, construction, field work, and other jobs whites considered inferior to them. Unless you owned a business, the chances of being hired in a decent paying job were slim to none—and slim was usually out of town.

The Death Of MLK

*"If we are to have peace on earth, our loyalties must become
ecumenical rather than sectional. Our loyalties must transcend our
race, our tribe, our class, and our nation and this means we must
develop a world perspective."*

MLK (Georgia 1963)

Obviously, changes in the workplace had to be made in Memphis, so a protest by sanitation workers brought national attention. The strike was nationally publicized, specifically in the presence of one of the world's most prolific leaders of equality. In 1968, Dr. Martin Luther led the sanitation efforts to seek higher wages. A march on city hall was a focal point of the demonstration. The event is often referred to as the "poor people's march."

Astonishingly, on April 4, 1968, Dr. King was gunned down as he stood on the second-floor balcony of the Lorraine Motel in Memphis, Tennessee. The ramifications from his death brought about a rampage of violence in over 100 cities. In Washington DC, an estimated twenty thousand people rioted. President Lyndon B. Johnson reacted by quickly deploying thirteen thousand federal and National Guard troops—many with fixed bayonets—to assist DC police in the attempt to restore order. It was the largest occupation of an American city by military forces since the civil war. When the city calmed down, four days later, the death toll was twelve and over a thousand people injured and more than six thousand arrests had been made. Over nine hundred stores and buildings were burned.

Meanwhile, the city of Memphis experienced looting, arson, and shooting minutes after Dr. King's death. Within a few hours, Tennessee National Guardsmen arrived to take control over street patrols in riot-torn Memphis. A twenty-four-hour general curfew was ordered. Travel was allowed only for emergency or health reasons. Schools, shops, and businesses were closed. Details concerning the curfew did not provide a definite end date.

In school, we were anguished about seeing one of our schoolmates on the news after being fatally gunned down by the policemen during the riot. Specifically, it was reported that Bobby Gains was in the act of looting in downtown Memphis. To this day, the specifics of Bobby's death have never been revealed. I guess the family did not think they had the legal support or right to pursue any wrongdoings involved with his death.

In retrospect, I decided to put my thoughts on paper to summarize Dr. King's tragedy.

The following poem flowed through my mind. I hope my thoughts and feelings do not offend anyone.

CALVIN KERR, JR.

The Teachings of a King

Once there was a man.
He had a dream.
He could see the future.
It surely seemed.

He taught us to gain
     peace and strength,
through nonviolence.
        Although his
        intentions
        were good, some
        people he could not
        convince.

He felt that one should
        not destroy
        happiness,
because of a racial
        thing.
        This was a critical lesson,
        in the teachings of a King.

He traveled many places,
east, west, north and
        south.
Everyone listened,
when he opened his
mouth.
"We shall overcome
Someday,"
        he would often
sing.
This song was like the
        anthem, in the
        teachings of a
King.

He often spoke of little
        white children,
and little black
        children,

joining hands
    together,
not being judged by
    their color,
but by the content of
    their character.

"I have been to the
    mountain top,"
he would shout,
while in the center
    ring.
The crowd responded
joyously,
acknowledging their
    belief in the
    teachings of a
    King.

He stood on a balcony
    that day.
The assassin did not
    miss.
He came to lead
sanitation
    workers,
for higher pay in
    Memphis.
No one realized,
the amount of violence
    and bloodshed
his death would bring.
Although he is gone,
the world will never
    forget
the teachings of a King,
Martin Luther.

CALVIN KERR, JR.

The death of Martin Luther King Jr. and others like Bobby helped fortify the unity that was created throughout the school. Mitchell Road High School's student population was relatively all African-American. I remember after the curfew ended, we conducted our own defiance of federal and local governments. We did it by our protest through "Black Mondays". "Black Mondays" meant that we would not attend school on Mondays. Yes, we called them Black Mondays to express our dissatisfaction in the way African-Americans and their institutions were unfairly treated throughout the nation during the '60s. We created our own version of protesting while utilizing the strategy of nonviolence. However, we were not the only students to use this method of protesting.

The Woolworth Sit-Ins

"Deeply sympathetic with the efforts of any group to enjoy the rights of equality that they are guaranteed by the Constitution."
President Eisenhower

A more nationally recognized sit-in movement featured a nonviolent strategy by the Greensboro Four. Although not the first sit-ins of the African-American civil rights movement, the Greensboro sit-ins were an instrumental action, leading to increased national sentiment at a crucial period in US history. The Greensboro sit-ins were a series of nonviolent protests which led to the Woolworth's department store chain reversing its policy of racial segregation in the southern United States. On February 1, 1960, four from the Agricultural and Technical College of North Carolina sat down at the lunch counter inside the Woolworth's store at 132 South Elm Street in Greensboro, North Carolina. Following the store policy, the lunch counter staff refused to serve the African-American men at the "whites only" counter and the store's manager asked them to leave. The four university freshman—Joseph McNeil, Franklin McCain, Ezell Blair Jr., and David Richmond—stayed until the store closed.

The next day, more than twenty African-American students, who had been recruited from other campus groups, came to the store to join the sit-in. White customers heckled black students, who read books and studied to keep busy. The lunch counter staff continued to refuse service.

Newspaper reporters and a TV cameraman covered the second day of peaceful demonstration, and others in the community learned of the protests. On the third day, more than sixty people came to the Woolworth's store. A statement was issued by the Woolworth's national headquarters, stating that the company would "abide by local custom" and maintain its segregated policy.

More than three hundred people took part on the fourth day. Organizers agreed to spread the sit-in protests to include the lunch counter at Greensboro's Kress store.

Soon after the Greensboro sit-in had begun, students in North Carolina towns launched their own sit-ins. Demonstrations spread to towns near Greensboro, including Winston-Salem, Durham, Raleigh, and Charlotte. Out-of-state towns like Lexington, Kentucky, also saw protests.

The movement then spread to other southern cities, including Richmond, Virginia; Nashville, Tennessee; where students of the Nashville Student Movement had been trained for a sit-in by civil rights activist James Lawson and had already started the process when Greensboro occurred. Although the majority of the protests were peaceful, there were instances where protests became violent. For example, in Chattanooga, Tennessee, tensions rose between black and whites and fights broke out. Another city where sit-ins occurred was Jackson, Mississippi. Students from Tougaloo College staged a sit-in on May 28, 1963. The sit-in is recorded in the autobiography of one of the members in attendance, Anne Moody. Moody described the treatment of the whites who were at the counter when they sat down, as well as the formation of the mob in the store, and how they finally managed to leave the store.

IMPACT

As sit-ins continued, tensions grew in Greensboro, and students began a far-reaching boycott of stores that had segregated lunch counters. Sales at the boycotted stores dropped by a third; this led to the store owners' abandonment of their segregated policies. Black employees of Greensboro's Woolworth's store were the first at the store's lunch counter on July 25, 1960. The next day, the entire Woolworth chain was desegregated, serving blacks and whites alike.

STAX RECORDS

The death of Dr. King not only brought about the rioting and chaos in major cities; some industries were affected by his death, too. Particularly, the disappearance of Stax studio to me was a strange phenomenon. Although the decline of Stax studio began after the death of Otis Redding, it carried on with the severance of the label's distribution deal with Atlantic Records in 1968. Prior to that Stax, to me, was the "Motown" of the south. It featured some of the greatest artists that the world would come to know. It was located at 925 E. McLemore Avenue, Memphis, Tennessee 38106. Before Dr. King's death, it was a melting pot for all types of people associated with the music industry, for many groups were mixed with blacks and whites. Although there were more, one of the mixed groups were Booker T. & the MG's. That group and many alike were the epitome of what Stax was about. Moreover, with the success of Booker T. & the MG's, Carla Thomas, The Mar-Keys, and Otis Redding, Stax studios became a magnet for other acts. Atlantic Records brought in two of their recording acts, the duo of Sam and Dave, to Memphis to record at Stax studio. Stax itself added William Bell, Eddie Floyd, the Mad Lads, and a top-notch producer and songwriter named Isaac Hayes and David Porter. In 1965, Stewart hired a very successful black Washington DC disc jockey named Al Bell as national sales. From the beginning, Al Bell took over the effective leadership of the company and greatly expanded its roster of artists. It was about the talent of the artists and not the color of their skin. I find it very ironic that the dissolution of Stax may have been in direct correlation with the death of MLK and his fight for equality. Needless to say, it is unfortunate that the world would never see Stax studio as an infamous recording studio that opened doors for blacks and whites again.

44TH PRESIDENT

Although the days of Stax Records as a studio and many of our black leaders are gone, I never imagined in all my lifetime that our nation would ever elect an African-American president. The seemingly impossible occurrence happened when Mr. Barack Obama was inaugurated the forty-fourth president of the United States of America. Days before his inauguration, thousands of people from all nations saturated areas of the White House, National Mall, and the Capitol Building, Washington Monument, Jefferson and Lincoln Memorials and other venues throughout DC. The inauguration of Barack Obama as the forty-fourth president of the United States took place on Tuesday, January 20, 2009. The inauguration, which set a record attendance for any event held in Washington, D.C., marked the commencement of the four-year term of Barack Obama as president and Joe Biden as vice president. Based on the combined numbers of attendance, television viewership, and Internet traffic, it was among the most observed events ever by the global audience. "A new birth of freedom," a phrase from the Gettysburg Address, served as the inaugural theme to commemorate the two hundredth anniversary of the birth year of Abraham Lincoln. In his speeches to the crowds, Obama referred to ideals expressed by Lincoln about renewal, continuity, and national unity. Obama mentioned these ideals in his speech to stress the need for shared sacrifice and a new sense of responsibility to answer America's challenges at home and abroad.

I will never forget the peaceful feeling I had inside the day before the inauguration, as it seemed to emulate the whole world. The calm atmosphere was enhanced by the behavior and attitude of people taking pictures with each other and assuring one another that we stand together as we embrace this change.

Strange Flame

Hey,
what is this strange
    black
    flame that warms
and
    lights the White
    House, today?

It burns not of oil or
    gas.
It is no replica of its
    past.
It is not pale.

CALVIN KERR, JR.

It is not frail.
It refuses to fail.
It is not of hell.
For all can tell,
It will prevail.

Hey,
what is this strange
     black
     flame that warms
and
     lights the White
     House, today?

Christians, Gentiles and
     Jews,
     Monks, Monarchs,
and
     Muslims, too
rich, poor, people like
     me
     and you,
all come to view.
It shines so bright.
All glows from its
light,
streets, cities,
     counties,
     and states.
It extends to foreign
     lands, continents
and
     all estates,

Hey,
what is this strange
     black
     flame that warms
and
     lights the White
     House, today?

It burns not of oil or
     gas.
It is no replica of its
     past.
It is not pale.
It is not frail.
It refuses to fail.
It is not of hell.
For all can tell,
It will prevail.

Hey,
what is this strange
     black
     flame that warms
and
     lights the White
     House, today?

From sea to shining sea,
it came to be.
It holds the key
     in the land of the
     free.
It gives all hope.
It uses no rope.
It is not dope,
nor a slippery slope.

Hey,
what is this strange
     black
     flame that warms
and
     lights the White
     House, today?

It burns not of oil or
     gas.
It is no replica of its
     past.

It is not pale.
It is not frail.
It refuses to fail.
It is not of hell.
For all can tell,
It will prevail.

Hey,
what is this strange
        black
        flame that warms
and
        lights the White
        House, today?

It is destined to be
        great.
It stands up straight,
It knows no hate,
nor does it
discriminate,
It is not insane,
'though it goes against
        the grain.
It knows its range.
It symbolizes change.

Hey,
what is this strange
        black
        flame that warms
and
        lights the White
        House, today?

It burns not of oil or
        gas.
It is no replica of its
        past.
It is not pale.
It is not frail.
It refuses to fail.

It is not of hell.
For all can tell,
It will prevail.

Hey,
what is this strange
     black
     flame that warms
and
     lights the White
     House, today?

Change!! Change! Change

CALVIN KERR, JR.

The MLK Memorial

Approximately three years later, I had the same feeling inside as I attended the dedication ceremony of the Martin Luther King Memorial on the banks of the Potomac, almost the center point in the triangle formed by the Washington Monument, Lincoln Memorial, and Jefferson Memorial. The Martin Luther King Jr. Memorial is located in West Potomac Park in Washington, D.C., southwest of the National Mall (but within the larger area commonly referred to as the National Mall). The memorial is America's 395th national park. The monumental memorial is located at the northwest corner of the tidal basin near the Franklin Delano Roosevelt Memorial, on a sightline linking the Lincoln Memorial to the northwest and the Jefferson Memorial to the southeast. The official address of the monument, 1964 Independence Avenue, SW, commemorates the year that the Civil Rights Act of 1964 became law. Covering four acres, the memorial opened to the public on August 22, 2011, after more than two decades of planning, fund-raising, and construction. A ceremony dedicating the memorial was scheduled for Sunday, August 28, 2011, the forty-eight anniversary of the "I Have a Dream" speech that Dr. Martin Luther King Jr. delivered from the steps of the Lincoln Memorial in 1963, but was postponed until October 16 (the 16th anniversary of the 1995 Million Man March on the National Mall) due to Hurricane Irene. Although this is not the first memorial to an African-American in Washington DC, Dr. King is the first African-American honored with a memorial on or near the National Mall and only the fourth non-president to be memorialized in such a way. The King Memorial is administered by the National Park Service (NPS). How appropriate of a location for a man who dedicated his life for equality on earth.

To start the day of the event, the chill of the early morning at sunrise was just cold enough for a light jacket or sweater. As we made our way to the subway, the first rays of the sun glared through the clouds of white and gray. Dreading the inconvenience of waiting to park, I had my wife drop me off before she left for work. Surprisingly, the subway's lot was not filled with cars as expected. I feared that the madden crowd, the mile or so walk, and the many hours of standing was still to come. The event was anticipated to draw more than a quarter million people. I am not sure if that number of people were in attendance as I never dreamed of sitting down. Not only was I able to sit down, but I managed to find a spot near the stage for the performances. The entire event highlighted by celebrities from all walks of life and culminated with words by the commander-in-chief was a tearjerker.

As I look back on my life, I realize how fortunate I was to leave Memphis as I did. I have been blessed with the fact of being a part of two utmost historical events an African American has ever encountered in a lifetime. I would be remised if I did not mention the times in Memphis when we, as black students at our school, decided to participate in Black Mondays due to the death of MLK; we used Black Mondays to shed light on all the inequities taking place in our world and others in the home of the free. Some of the inequities included are fair wages, school facilities and equipment, employment, law enforcement, and public facilities.

Although not as profanely obvious, the struggle for equal rights continues. Federal and state governments can pass all the mandates in the world, but they don't mean a thing unless a lot of ignorant Americans change the hate ingrained in their minds.

CHAINED 2 DA' PORCH

AT GUNPOINT

Without suspicion and before I could say another word, he pressed the open barrel of a 9mm Smith and Weston firmly against the right side of my face. This was the fourth time in my life I became fearful of death, and in two of those incidences, my husband (ex) was the offender. Terrified, I pleaded, "Please don't kill me." A moment later, my son appeared. My ex tried to hide the pistol. Quickly, I jumped out of the car. A bit bolder, I dared him, "If you are going to shoot me, it will have to be in the back," as I walked away from the car. Realizing what was happening, my son insisted, "Dad, give me the gun." My ex lied about not having a gun. My son replied, "I can tell by the look in Mom's eyes that she is not lying so give me the gun." Unwillingly, he gave it up. Once again, my life was spared with the aid of one of my children, and this time it was one of my twelve-year-old twins.

Drama with the pistol began when I needed someone to watch one of my twin boys. I wanted to go shopping to buy him a pair of shoes. My mind must have had a sudden brain cramp as I decided to let my ex watch my son. Finished with my shopping, I called my ex to ensure my son was ready to be picked up. He indicated that my son was not quite ready. When I arrived at my ex's apartment, I was in a hurry, and I could not understand what was taking so long. Unpleasant words were exchanged between my ex and me. My feistiness must have triggered a bit of anger within him; however, it should not have led him to do anything harmful to me. Nonetheless, as he walked down a flight of stairs, I noticed he hid something under his shirt. He opened the car door and eased into the car with me. At that moment, he pressed the pistol against my face. My fear of death has always been rooted deeper than with my life being taken away. The first question that comes to mind is, "What will happen to my children?"

NIGHTMARE ON EASTER SUNDAY

Believe it or not, I was even closer to death the first time he tried to kill me. It all started on a bright sunny and beautiful Easter Sunday. So nervous and anxious, I did not want anything to interfere with my plans. It was my idea and I worked hard in preparation for an Easter program. How can people not enjoy themselves? I had it all figured out. The only thing that I needed was a little money from my husband. As usual, he did not bother to show up that Friday—payday weekend. He was gone for two days. I wanted to tie up the loose ends by purchasing inexpensive items needed for my big day. Twenty-five dollars would suffice. Most of the money was to buy white shirts for my twin boys. I ended up borrowing it from my friend, Iris.

As soon as my husband arrived that Easter morning, I confronted him for the twenty-five dollars to pay Iris. I smelt he would be a problem. I never visualized it would lead to a near-fatal endeavor. Once I realized that he was under the influence of drugs or alcohol, I tried to separate myself from him. With a sense of urgency, I ran out of the room to his mother. I thought her presence would defuse his radical behavior. I hid behind her as she persuaded him to calm down.

When I felt everything was cool, I made my way to the kitchen. He followed me and he started up again. A pot of boiling grits was on the stove; grabbing them, I made a gesture to throw them at him. Moments later, his mother appeared in the kitchen. She recognized his intentions of wanting to hurt me, so she yelled at him to stop. He got really ugly with her, and he had the look of a man possessed by demons. I knew I had to completely separate myself from him. I made a frantic run for the front door, but he beat me to it. While outside the house, he disabled the car by snatching a wire from the engine compartment. He chased me around the car until I decided to run back into the house.

In the house, his mother was yelling at him, trying to get him to stop. But his nephew, Rodney, who was staying with us, did not want to get involved, so he did not let me in his room.

Once again, I made a break for the kitchen area. My husband caught me and threw me onto the kitchen table. When I hit the table, the various colors of dye for the Easter eggs went airborne. They splattered all over the floor. Desperately, I tried to get away without success. Although I was about three feet from the door, I could not escape his grip. He was just too strong for me. Initially, he beat me with his fist, then he pulled a hammer out of the nearby utility closet and struck me in the back of my head with it. I was in misery and in a vast amount of pain. I kicked and kicked, attempting to crawl away. He struck my legs so hard and so often they turned black and blue. He went back to striking my head with the hammer.

Somehow, I got up, only to slip and fall back to the floor from the water and the dye. If you ever saw the episode of the movie *Carrie* when Cicely Spacek was drenched with a bucket of blood at her prom, you can picture how I looked. The rainbow colors from the dye, my blood, my tears, and bruises turned me into a pitiful mess (for lack of any other way I could describe myself). Just when I thought it could not get any worse, he wrapped a cord around my neck. My poor babies witnessed it all, and by that time, they had to be traumatized. All of their screaming and crying got his attention, and he stopped beating me. Now, I knew I was at the brink of death. I was very bloody as I continued to lose blood. I never felt so much pain in all my life.

Finally, my daughter called the police. When the police found me, I was lying on the floor with my husband still beside me. He had just released the cord from around my neck. The beating with the hammer, the choking with the cord, the brutal licks with his fist, and the amount of blood I lost all made me helpless, and all I could do was lie there. It was the first time in my life I felt as if I was going to die. To add insult to injury, as I was gaining my consciousness, my husband was lying to the police about catching me with another man when he came home. Simultaneously, the ambulance workers tried to diagnose and sustain me. They wanted to take me to the emergency room, but all I could mutter was, "I want my mother."

After numerous inquiries, the authorities released me to my mother, and she took me to her house. Making use of all the remedies she could think of to revive me, she soaked me in the tub. Afterward, she rubbed my body down with some sort of ointment. She fed me like a baby. In other words, my mother was my savior as she nursed me back to health. However, I do not think she ever forgave me for marrying that man.

My mother's intuition tried to warn me not to marry him. I kept my pregnancy a secret, so she did not know my reason. I thought everything would be all right after the birth of my baby girl. I did not expect to have another child by him. But, unexpectedly, I got pregnant again. Before the twins came, our marriage was on the edge. It did not take long for it to fall apart, especially because he was leaving home all the time and spending up the rent money, not to mention the physical and mental abuse I endured. I never thought I would hate him to the point of denying him my body. It has to be the most degrading and nastiest feeling in the world to have a man force himself inside you.

Trapped Inside My Fears

I can feel the walls
    close in on me.
The chains and balls
    weighs heavy on my feet.

I began to cry.
Why am I in such a bad state of
    mind?
Who am I?
Why is life so unkind?

Sometimes I use my kids as a
crush.
I just want them to be safe,
because I love them so much,
We've got to leave this
    forsaken place.

Today, I will change this life I
    live.
The focus of my big picture is
    clear.
For this man, I have no more love
    to give.
I have learned my lessons
throughout these years.

I refuse to stay trapped inside my
        fears.
I ain't going to shed no more
tears, no more tears.
I refuse to stay trapped inside my
        fears.

There are so many times,
I am knocked down to the floor.
I can count the days when things
        are fine.
I cannot take this hurt anymore.

I am in such a craze.
Hour after hour, I stand on my
feet.
There are so many days,
I can't eat and I can't sleep.
My hardship doesn't range from 9
to 5.
As I pray to the heavens above,
I thank God for the 24/7/365 he
        keeps me alive,
            and most of all for His love.

Today, I will change this life I
        live.
The focus of my big picture is
        clear.
For this man, I have no more love
        to give.
I have learned my lessons
throughout these years.
I refuse to stay trapped inside my
        fears.
I ain't going to shed no more
tears, no more tears.
I refuse to stay trapped inside my
        fears.

I have managed to save
        a few nickels and dimes in my
        account.
He will rant and rave,

if he ever found out.
I plan to leave
    in the middle of the night.
He will be fast asleep,
    when we take our flight.

Today, I will change this life I
    live.
The focus of my big picture is
    clear.
For this man, I have no more love
    to give.
I have learned my lessons
throughout these years.
I refuse to stay trapped inside my
    fears.
I ain't going to shed no more
tears, no more tears.
I refuse to stay trapped inside my
    fears.

Somehow, I had to get away from him. My children were not going to grow up in this hostile environment. They needed to know that this was not the norm. My plan of putting away money without him knowing worked. Getting a gauge of my pennies one day, I had enough for the security deposit and three months of rent. Quietly, in the middle of the night, I got the kids out of bed. All the packing was done previously, so all I had to do was get them in the car. With that accomplished, I fled for Memphis. When my ex found out my whereabouts, he did the unexpected. He moved to Memphis also and made promises after promises. Finally, he wooed me back into his life only to make my life even more stressful.

The episode on Easter was the bell that brought me out of hypnosis. He stalked and haunted me. Until one day, Papa Joe Kool caught him in the act by my place. He told my ex to take a walk with him. Papa Joe Kool must have made him an offer he could not refuse because he never bothered me again. Needless to say, marrying him was my biggest mistake ever. By the grace of God, I am still alive and divorced.

I BECAME A JUNKIE

Staying alive did not come so easy for me, especially in conceiving my twin boys. In direct correlation conceiving them, I had to have three operations. The doctors cut me around the left side of my abdomen, and they also cut-up my vagina pretty good, making it impossible for me to naturally have children again. The pain of the operations was so unbearable that I could not eat. I became a junkie. All I wanted was the pain medication to make me feel better. I was shot so much that the nurses ran out of places to shoot me. I got to the point where I began shooting myself anywhere I could find a spot. I was desperate, and I really believed that I was going to die; therefore, I took care of all the legalities such as wills, insurances, and all other necessary paperwork.

I gave up. If my primary doctor had not brought in a specialist from New York City, I feel most certain that I would be dead today. After my third operation, slowly but surely, I began to come back to life. My struggle lasted approximately five months. The pain of the operation caused me to become introverted. Like a homeless person that slept on a park bench, I neglected my body. The nest atop my head was meshed together, and my body was not that of the 110 pound woman everyone had come to know. One day, a glimpse in the mirror reflected a shameful being looking back at me. The nurse felt sorry for me, and she took the first step in putting me back together. Little by little, she unwove the nest and made it resemble hair.

The nurse mending my hair and the thing staring back at me in the mirror somehow brought me out of a daze, and I wanted to live again. The small steps I took to return to a healthy life started with a crawl. The path from my room to the nurse's station and beyond other doors became my track. My routine took place after hours, so the coast was always clear. Privacy was important to me.

Eventually, I left the hospital healthy, yet I found myself weighing 180 pounds. When you are not recognized by your friends in public because of your weight, it is time to do something about it. Walking not only helped me to lose weight, but it improved my strength and stamina. I began to feel like my old self again. Gradually, my self-esteem improved, and I took back control of my own life.

PAPA JOE KOOL

The only other time I ever feared for my life occurred with my father. In the community, he was nicknamed Papa Joe Kool. He had a reputation of being overly protective when it came to his girls. His strict rules and treatment was borderline child abuse. His domineering attitude and behavior reined over our household with fear. It impacted all our lives. The three of us could not wait to reach the point where we could leave home for good. Linda and I received most of the beatings. Millie got out of a lot of stuff because she was the youngest. Each one of us had a brutal moment with him. However, as I reminisce about Millie's and my worst confrontations with him, those were as soft as a feather compared to that of Linda's.

Linda's nightmares occurred while having a waistline party to raise money. The money was to fund her trip to Mexico. We never envisioned the price Linda would pay, although my mother was the ring leader. She even collected the money.

Anyway, the party was swinging and everyone was dancing and having fun. We were letting the good times roll just when Papa Joe Kool pulled up. We were startled because we never expected to see him home this early. Immediately, he transformed into a raging bull.

It was as though Linda wore red because she was his target, especially after he ran everybody out of the house and some boy she had been dancing with yelled her name from the street. Papa grabbed Linda and began to strangle her. My mother intervened to keep him from killing her. I just wanted the nightmare to be over. That incident was only one of the numerous situations we had to encounter living in the household with Papa Joe Kool.

Aunt Cile And Cynethia

How did we get to this point? As the story is told by my Aunt Cile, my mother's family migrated from Natchez, Mississippi, in the '60s. It was a small town located near the gulf, approximately an eight-to ten-hour driving distance south of Memphis. My grandmother, Stella Bivens, owned a three-room house with an outhouse toilet behind it. A well stood in front of it. With no running water, they had a pump. All In all, nine aunts and uncles lived in this quaint, antiquated house, roughly furnished with a wood-burning stove. The stove was used for cooking and heating.

Aunt Lucy (Cile) was the oldest, and she was the first who flew the coop. In flight, she flew with plenty of baggage.

Particularly, her skin was so light that she could pass for a Caucasian. She landed in the vicinity of DC. Mainly, because of her skin color, she could get high-paying jobs because she dated unsuspecting white men. With the money she made, she was able to send some home, or she would bring it when she came.

Once she got caught up in her game, she would return to Natchez and on to Memphis so she could not be found. Moreover, she opened a café in North Memphis. It was called Lucy. She purchased her first home in Memphis as well. Established, she returned to Natchez and brought back Andrea. Andrea was about ten years old. Aunt Cile provided the means for her education. After my mother Andrea was educated, Aunt Cile went back for Sue.

Sue must have had a white baby daddy and a black baby daddy because one of her daughters could pass for white and the other was dark skinned. For numerous reasons, those two girls along with me and my sisters grew up together.

During my teenage years, I could not understand why my father overwhelmingly mistrusted and controlled us in such a harsh way. I guess fathering three daughters had a lot to do with him managing his household like Alcatraz. He may have drawn parallel to what his mischief as a young man resulted in, having a child out of wedlock. Whatever it was, I must say it drove me to the point of leaving and never wanting to return home again. Another incident involving my cousin, Cynethia, may have played a part in his demeanor.

Cynethia, like Aunt Cile, had a light complexion with freckles. She could almost past for white. In her teens, she was already playing games with men for money. She would have two or three men on the hook at a time. I always asked her, "Cynethia, why can't you be satisfied with one man?" Yet, she kept sneaking and sleeping around until she ended up getting pregnant at the age of fifteen. She wanted to marry the father who was about twenty-two years old. Because of her age, Cynethia could not sign the marriage paperwork, and her mother would not sign for her.

DWAYNE'S DEATH

The very day she turned sixteen, Cynethia married Dwayne Hunt. Dwayne loved her very dearly. He worked hard doing everything in his power to provide for her. Obviously, it was not enough to satisfy her lust for money and her spending habits. Therefore, Cynethia continued to turn tricks. Dwayne left out of the front door and her pimp came in through the back. This went on for a while until Dwayne left for work one day and doubled back. He walked right into the pimp's bullet. Tales of that incident was not only in the newspapers but circulated through neighborhoods and the high school we attended.

The dynamics of the incident impacted many families. Cynethia could not stay in her own home because it was being bombarded with bricks. Glass windows were being knocked out every day by Dwayne's sisters and friends. With all that going on, my mother made her come stay with us because we did not live in that neighborhood. It did not take long for people to find out she lived with us. That move placed our lives in jeopardy. Someone at school threatened me every day. I lost a lot of respect from people who were close to me. Nonetheless, I still had real friends who were willing to help me fight. Even at Dwayne's funeral, my sisters, cousins, other relatives, and I were being assaulted and threatened.

Before the funeral, Papa Joe Kool visited Dwayne's father. He tried to reason with Dwayne's father to no avail. My father's point was that because of Cynethia's age, Dwayne should not have been involved with her nor married her in the first place. My father was not very empathetic. He could not understand the man's frustration of losing his only son. Their differences almost caused a fight in Mr. Hunt's front yard. Time was the only element that calmed the feud between the families and their friends.

Although the flame from the fallout out of Dwayne's death was pretty smothered out, our father never let up on us. It may have intensified Papa Joe Kool's warden-like behavior. Literally, one could not see the balls and chains that burdened us through our childhood year. We were mentally bruised by the weight. I now refer to it as being chained to the porch.

MY HIGH SCHOOL SWEETHEART

Linda, Millie, and I (Carolyn) were the children that Joe and Andrea Lawson have together. Linda was the oldest. When she graduated from high school, she was at Tennessee State a year before me. She acted very maturely. She schooled me on how I would have to handle men. She told me that I would not run into many men like my high school boyfriend.

My high school boyfriend had been extremely patient with me. From all the nasty comments my father made about boys, I would constantly push him away when he wanted to get intimate with me. Once, he bought me the most beautiful watch for my birthday. Outraged, my father demanded for me to give it back. That was one time I defied him. My mother took my side when he ridiculed me. He yelled, "All he wants to do is get into your panties." To my surprise, my mother answered, "I do not care what his intentions are. You need to leave them alone." His despitefulness haunted us. We were always in his shadows. On my boyfriend visits, restlessly, he paced throughout the house. One night as my boyfriend waited for his ride, Papa Joe Kool informed him, "It is getting late. It is time for you to go." Politely Craig said, "Yes, sir," extended his goodbyes and walked out the door. It was an extremely dark night and the corner store was miles from our house for him to make a call. I didn't know if he even had a dime for a phone call. I barely slept a wink from worrying about his safety. Why didn't I at least try to convince my father to allow him to stay until his brother arrived?

My reluctant attitude to embrace and show him some love would come back to haunt me. That along with problems at home and the way my father treated him made his decision to join the military easier. Before he joined, he took me to our high school prom. I believe my mother was just as happy as I was. She cherished that occasion. Her face glowed all the time she took pictures of us. She would hold on to those pictures for years. Going to the prom with Craig was the highlight of my high school days.

It was shortly after graduation Craig joined the military. Initially, we wrote to each other back and forth. In my heart, he was the only person that I ever wanted to love. So naïve, I thought that we would always be together. For unknown reasons, other people disliked our relationship. Someone succeeded in breaking us up after Craig received an anonymous letter lying on me. The writer indicated that I had sex with him. I did not find that out until Craig was on leave and came to Nashville to see me. I was so nervous, but I had made my mind up that tonight is the night that I would let him make love to me. Before we could get intimate, he told me the story concerning the letter. We argued and he informed me that once he left the motel room I would never see him again. I tried to convince him that I was still a virgin and I waited for him. He was so angry that he never heard a word I said. After him, I was so broken-hearted it took me several years before I dated and met my ex. Craig and I never communicated again for over forty years.

The Ravishment Of Millie

While I had my problems trusting men, Millie had problems of her own. She was the most beautiful one among the three of us. Before she reached high school, her breasts were twice as big as mine. Her figure was like a Coca-Cola bottle. Her legs were big and sexy. She was fair-skinned with freckles. Her clothes fitted in such a way to showcase her sexy body. Needless to say, she never had a problem finding a boyfriend or man. Her problem was keeping them from bothering her. Usually, when she did open up, it was with older men. She could melt a man with one look into her eyes.

Her beauty turned out to be her downfall from the grace and her mental stability that she once flaunted. It was an incident with someone she knew. He lured her to a location and he and one of his friends raped her. After that tragic occurrence, Millie would never be the same.

Millie's Fate

One of the ramifications of the rape was that Millie became an introvert. She lived alone and did not want anyone to enter her space. From time to time, I checked on her to ensure that she was okay. One day, I received a call from her case worker. Her case worker informed me that the landlord was about to put Millie out. She had fallen behind in her rent. Dumbfounded, I asked the case worker why I wasn't notified before the situation became a crisis. From her response, I could tell that she dropped the ball somewhere down the line. To make a long story short, I had to make room for Millie at the place where I was staying. My plans were for us to stay put for a while to save money before we moved to a more accommodating place. Besides, I wanted to get away from the person I was staying with anyway. Millie smiled at the fact that it would just be me and her. We had it all planned until one day I heard her scream from her room. Frantically, I ran into her room and I realized that she had fallen. She appeared dizzy, and I immediately took her to the nearest emergency room. At first, everything seemed to be going well and I did not receive any negative feedback from the doctor. Feeling relieved, I decided to go get us some breakfast.

By the time I got back to the clinic, the medical personnel were in panic mode. The blood thinners they gave her caused a vein or an artery to burst. Now, the facility did not have the equipment or capability to sustain her. They had to medically evacuate her to another hospital. Once we arrived at the general hospital, I could not believe it when the doctor informed me that biologically, Millie was dead. I became hysterical with the thought that my younger sister practically died in my arms. I questioned myself, "What else could I do?"

The one thing I leaned on was that Craig and I spoke throughout the whole ordeal. He encouraged me to be strong. He reassured me that there was nothing else I could have done. His words were, "You cannot blame yourself. Please stay calm and rational. You have so many things to do, and you need your health to do them." He went on to say, "You have a lot of life left and Millie would want you to enjoy it. Remember, those are the type of things you and her talked about. I love you." Hearing his voice and knowing that he was concerned for my welfare helped me maintain some sense of composure. I needed that type of encouragement. I thank God that he could provide the inspiration that I needed at that time. The words, "You have a lot of life left, and Millie would want you to enjoy it," stayed on my mind and helped me to endure the funeral.

THE REUNION

In retrospect, Craig had been out of my life for about forty years. We restored our friendship a year prior to Millie's death. I suddenly received a phone call while shopping at Wal-Mart. He started the conversation in secrecy after I answered and he confirmed it was me. I did not recognize his voice at first, so I became irritated when I asked, "Who is this?" He responded, "You do not know who this is?" I said, "No, and how did you get this number?" I do not give my number out to just anyone. Toying with me, he insisted, "You knew me before." When he made that statement, finally, I recognized his voice. Excitedly, I yelled, "I know you, Craig Jones. How are you doing?" Grinning, he said, "I am good now that you did not hang up on me." We talked for a while about our teenage moments, such as going into a hotel room. Neither one of us knew where to start. We would just sit there and talk. Those were precious times to me because I was assured that he loved me beyond having sex with me. At the end of our conversation, he gave me several contact numbers. After that initial phone call, he was all I could think of along with all the innocence and kindness we had in our relationship. It took me a while to gain the courage to return his call. I was afraid that I would not be able to hold back my feelings for him. No matter how long it had been, I still had a warm spot in my heart for this man. Whenever I spoke to him, I cautioned myself to not reveal my true feelings for him.

During one conversation, to turn him off a little bit, I told him I looked the same except that I picked up a little weight. I knew we were destined to meet. Through one of our conversations, I learned that he was driving from near Baltimore to Smyrna beach on business. His plan was to return to Baltimore via Memphis. From Memphis, he had to see about his land in Arkansas. As he drove to Smyrna, I kept in touch with him to ensure he did not fall asleep. I was so nervous from the anticipation of seeing him. He was in Memphis for two days prior to my meeting with him in his sister's house. The moment I saw him, I could not hold back when he almost looked the same. Quickly, I rushed to his arms and told him to give me a kiss. Remembering the last time I saw him, I informed him, "You owe me an apology." He looked confused as he responded, "For what?" Dazed from looking into his eyes, I muttered, "For not believing me in the hotel room forty years ago when I told you I was a virgin." "Well," he stated, "we will discuss that over dinner."

We decided to have dinner downtown near Beale Street. It was a very rainy night, but I never knew the rain was there. I felt so good inside, I could not eat. I wanted to cherish the feeling. He opened doors for me. At one moment, he ended up holding the door for a group of ladies as they scurried into a building out of the rain. I heard one say, "He is such a well-mannered and handsome gentleman." Then another questioned, "Is that your husband?" Smiling, I lied, "Yes, he is my husband." For that night, I wanted the world to know that he was mine.

From a distance, we keep a very strong and healthy relationship. Sometimes I visit him and Linda in the Baltimore area since they both live there. Craig and I may coordinate our vacation time in Smyrna Beach, Florida, when he comes to visit his family members who live in Memphis. I must admit I am having the best times of my life.

But I reminisce about the many volatile experiences that haunted me throughout my life; today, I feel a calm resolve within myself. With inspiration from my sister (Linda), who has moved back to Memphis, and Craig, I am almost to the point of complete makeover, both mentally and physically. Additionally, I have noticed a transformation in Linda. We are the only two left from our immediate family, so we have vowed to support each other even more than we did in the past. As kids, we had to support each other because we were the ones most subject to being chained to the porch.

So, gone are the days of being raped and beaten by my ex. Gone are the days I could barely feed and clothe my three children. Gone are the days I wished I could die because of all the pain from my surgery. Gone are the days Linda and I were almost beaten to death by Papa Joe Kool. Gone are the days of being chained 2 da' porch.

WHOSE LIFE IS IT, ANYWAY

Being A DI In 'Bama

When I arrived at the hospital, she was lying there with intravenous sedation (IV) in her arm. Oh, how I wanted to snatch out the IV. I thought about the precious hours I spent training her to graduate. It seemed as though she intentionally timed her attempt simultaneously with my commander's briefing. My co-drill instructor interrupted us to inform me of her intentions. If my black behind had any chance of turning red, that would have been the moment. It did not matter that she was one in thousands of trainees I had the opportunity to train because she was like a personal project to me. She was my first female challenge of the cycle (a group of privates going through training at the same time), although two male cycles did proceed the female cycle.

I was almost halfway through a two-year DI (drill instructor) stint at a post located almost half the distance between Atlanta, Georgia, and Birmingham, Alabama. Being an African-American male in Alabama was already a black mark against me, and I had to withstand an array of nightmares. Complicating problems more dynamically was an American Legion club standing right outside the main gate of the fort. The kicker was that Blacks were not allowed in the club (this was the late 80s). For that reason, it was off-limits to all military personnel. Do you think that the club's atmosphere was a microcosm of many establishments in Alabama?

The life of a DI can be very stressful and frustrating without discrimination. It seemed to fester on to the post. On a daily basis, I faced it along with the rigors of the six to eight weeks of boot camp. The undue pressure was a burden because boot camp entails the utmost level of responsibility. Every cycle is an adventure featuring a diverse company of men and women. Each day of training has the potential to end in tragedy. From the time the privates are greeted on the bus until they are physically transferred into their respective platoons, it is a challenge. Therefore, the DI has many restless hours. The long, hot days can cause injuries, from heat exhaustion to heat stroke, while the dark, cold nights can cause frostbite and anything up to pneumonia. At the extreme, both may lead to death. I reiterate everything to include the training, care, and safeguarding of trainees—they are in the hands of the DI.

Typically, as with all soldiers, it is highly pertinent that a DI practice the following leadership traits: bearing, courage (physical and moral), decisiveness, dependability, endurance, enthusiasm, initiative, integrity, judgment, justice, knowledge, loyalty, tact, and unselfishness. Practicing the aforementioned characteristics can definitely help to lessen the likelihood of breaking rules and regulations. One of the most prevalent crimes that a DI commits is fraternization, particularly with female privates.

Apparently, the temptation of getting involved with a beautiful female cadet overwhelmed many DIs, for many have lost their rank, hat, and patch. The utmost of the punishments is a court-martial or a dishonorable discharge.

DI MORTON

DI Morton lost his rank, patch, and hat. Being assigned to the company ahead of me, he was one of my former subordinates in a medical clinic. Our acquaintance took place well before his marriage.

Prior to becoming a DI, he got divorced. Definitely, it was a surprise to me simply because he and his ex-wife had a beautiful child. His wife was gorgeous as well. She, too, was a soldier - a Caucasian with beautifully tanned skin. I suspected the divorce stemmed from his extra-marital activities. As soon as their marriage fell apart, she became interested in an army officer. When that happened, he would talk to me about her for hours. Many times, he was liquored up, but still, I allowed him the time to vent.

Eventually, he would cut down on his woeful moods. The fact he was a bit of a lady's man helped. Confidence in his ability to woo a female was never a problem for him. His fair complexion overshadowed a few zits on his face. Bo-legged, he stood about five feet ten inches tall, and he was well-conditioned.

By the time I got on the trail, he was already involved with another female soldier. Marriage to her was soon insinuated. I tried to use tact in telling him I did not like the idea. How could I tell him the truth about her? I made a huge mistake one morning as I barged into a fellow DI's room. I thought I was shaking and harassing the DI. I yelled, "Boy, if you do not get your butt up out of that bed right now, I will throw you out!" When the person turned over, with head and face uncovered, right then, I realized it was someone I was not supposed to see. She responded by saying, "DI Britton is in the shower." After that incident, DI Morton constantly relayed to me that his wife "to be" could not stand DI Britton. I kept that secret because I was a friend to both. I felt it was not my business. Besides, DI Morton's involvement with his fiancé would keep him occupied to the point of avoiding fraternization with trainees. So I thought. In retrospect, he displayed signs. I should have recognized those red flags. One indication was when he would allow the privates to flirt with him. There are numerous methods he could have used to deter their behavior.

Another clue was that he constantly volunteered for Charge of Quarters (CQ) duty. Often, he relieved DIs of CQ duty without charging them. Something had to be up because the duty required one to stay at the barracks with the privates the entire night. In doing so, the opportunity to engage in affairs with privates was there for him. None of the previously mentioned signs were concrete proof of him misbehaving. However, material evidence came to fruition through the mail. A private wrote him a letter and somehow the "head shed" found out about it. The company commander was one who always looked for discrepancies in order to hang a DI. It was like a trophy for her. Additionally, the first sergeant was not any better. He reminded me of the Pee Wee Herman character with no backbone at all. In other words, a DI did not stand a chance in their company. They ate DI Morton alive. They stripped him of everything. He swore up and down, defending his position by saying, "I did not know she was going to write me. There was nothing in the letter implicating fraternization."

DI Morton was not the only DI to fraternize with a female trainee on post or at an army installation. One of the most notorious stories was created by the goings-on of DIs at a military installation north of Baltimore. Disgracefully, I knew the DIs and company commander there. It was beyond my active duty career. I served as an army instructor at the high school level. I conducted a drill competition, and I used the DIs from that very company to score the meet. I had no clue that they would ever have committed such dreadful acts, although I was well aware of the struggling survival and the discomforts of being a DI. It was even more when the company was composed of female trainees.

Furthermore, it was hard trying to abide by technical and physical parameters. Mind you, it can be very difficult to take care of some privates, especially if they are not the brightest color in the rainbow. Private (PVT) Shenet was one of those privates. The amount of push-ups he could do correctly when he first came to basic was zero. He could not walk and chew bubble gum at the same time. When I yell "PVT Shenet, front and center," the calamity begins. From the first step, his canteen falls off of his pistol belt. As he bends down to pick up the canteen, he loses his ammunition pouch. With another step, his first aid pouch hits the ground. By the time he stands in front of me, he is holding all the field equipment in his arms. I am fuming and shaking my head as I curse the recruiter who enlisted him.

The safety requirements were designed for trainees like Shenet. Depending on the training, a specific number of DIs had to be present, particularly on firing ranges when live rounds are actually fired. Qualification with the M16 rifle was mandatory for all trainees to graduate from basic training. The minimum standard was hitting twenty-three out of forty targets. Therefore, numerous hours of practice are spent on the ranges.

A peculiar thing happened to a private on one of the rifle ranges. Although he may have been nervous, I dismissed his mishap as possibly a food product in disagreement with his stomach. His problem occurred right before the range was cleared for live fire. Very discreetly, he informed me that he had accidentally unloaded his breakfast. Immediately, I sent him to the latrine. I allowed him to take as much time as he needed. Additionally, I wanted him to let me know if he needed soap and water. I realized that his canteen may not have provided him with enough water to clean up. As you can see, there are times the DI must be empathetic. I did not want to add to his uncomfortable feeling, especially on a live fire range.

Again, the long days and nights can become very tiresome and hectic. Even the required number of DIs cannot prevent some of the fatal tragedies. Specifically, on one occasion, when a private took his own life, the DIs had no chance of preventing it. Who could see it coming? It happened so suddenly. Without suspicion, the private took the rifle and placed it under his chin. Immediately, he pulled the trigger. The non-piercing material of the Kevlar helmet he wore caused the bullet to rattle around inside it. According to eyewitnesses, the bullet scrambled his brains, head and face areas. Almost daily, potential incidences, such as this one, places the DIs, trainees, and all personnel involved lives in jeopardy.

COVER GIRL

In direct correlation with the potential of something fatal to happen daily, DIs must maintain control through discipline. Fortunately, DIs maintain a lot of control through discipline; however, many like DI Morton throw discipline out the window when it comes to fraternization. As a young man, it is very easy to place yourself in compromising positions with female subordinates.

Out of all the female subordinates to approach me, only one really made me have second thoughts. It was not uncommon for me to use the push-up to keep them out of my face, especially on "Cover Girl," who was a reservist from Baton Rouge, Louisiana. The other privates gave her the nickname because of her modeling career. She shared with them pictures from a fashion magazine, and of course, she was on the cover.

The glow of Cover Girl illuminated my entire platoon. Her beauty was matched only by her character. One of the most gorgeous black women I had ever met; she, too, was mentally and physically strong. She did whatever it took to get the job done. Moreover, she helped the other girls in the platoon. After late night training, Cover Girl took the time to dress other privates' hair. At breakfast, they looked as though they just stepped out of a beauty salon. I took heat for that. Once, DI James stated, "DI Houston, how is it that all your girls have their hair fixed and looking fresh? You must take them to get their hair done after training." I tried to play it off when I replied, "I am just as mystified as you are." My suspicion was that Cover Girl used a pen light at night to fix their hair.

Throughout my years on the trail, she was the only private that I pulled the reins on because she volunteered for almost every detail. It did not matter how many push-ups I made her do, she kept asking for more. As I did with all trainees, when I needed to place emphasis on a point I wanted to make, I used push-ups. Sometimes trainees would owe me thousands of push-ups. Their bills had to be paid up before they graduated. Cover girl always paid up immediately. I remember the one time she finally broke down and cried. Unknowingly, I made her push until someone informed me that she hurt herself while on detail. Boy, did I feel like a jackass. Talk about breaking her down, afterward, I found myself unable to look her straight in the eyes. When I did look her in the eyes, I felt apologetic.

A more negative encounter involving the same female cycle was yet to occur. When the bus pulled up to the barracks, I was the first one on to greet them. I stood about six feet two inches tall, and I weighed approximately 185 pounds. After the cycle was over, one of the girls informed me that when she first met me, she thought I was the blackest, ugliest, and meanest thing she had ever seen in her life. I recalled stepping on the bus, and in a loud and stern voice, I yelled, "Let me have your attention. I am Drill Sergeant James Houston. Welcome to your new home for approximately the next eight weeks." I heard a slight noise, so I reiterated, "I said let me have your attention. This is not Burger King where you can have it your way. This is Charlie Company. I want everybody to get off the bus. Once off the bus, you will form one line in an orderly manner and grab all your bags. You must grab every bag you brought with you at once because you ain't coming back to the bus." I knew many would have a hard time carrying their bags because of the number of bags they brought. I made an example of a little skinny one who brought the most. Oh, how she struggled. With every step, she dropped a bag, and every time she dropped a bag, my onion-smelling breath was dead in her face. "You better get that bag off of my dirt. Where did you think you were going anyway? This is not a vacation, and this ain't the beach. You will not see the outside of these gates for eight weeks."

THINKS LIKE ME

The next eight weeks would be a drill instructor's nightmare, especially for me. This happened to be my second full cycle of trainees. I was still getting acquainted with my fellow DIs and the command staff. Many of the DIs could not stand me because I was the highest ranking sergeant first class (SFC) on post. I understood the white haters, but I could not quite get it when I felt slighted by blacks.

There were at least two black DIs I did not trust. One was an arrogant woman military policewoman with a suspicious nature. She knew that she was the finest woman on earth, to the extent that she felt every man could not help but want her. But she was married. I must confess, she did have a certain flair, a nice butt, and looked cute riding around in her canary yellow Chevrolet Corvette. But I could not stand her and our personalities clashed. Covertly, she tried to set me up for failure.

She would be huddled with my assistant DI when I walked in our office sometimes. I never thought anything of it until, one day, her husband dropped by. He accused them of having an affair. He mentioned it to me. Although I did not like her, I never told him about their meetings. In turn, I spoke with my assistant. Of course, he denied it.

I could have used that opportunity to get back at her because I suspected that she instructed the company commander (CO) to conduct a urinalysis on our unit. It was right after I came off leave. We had a very casual conversation. I told her that I almost had too much fun. It was a good thing I used only alcohol because she took the opportunity to convince the CO to conduct a urinalysis to bust me. She and the CO had an excellent relationship—neither liked me, so, constantly, I had to watch my back.

Even with a black First Sergeant (1SG), I had to watch my back. He was not exactly against me, but he listened to lies from the other DIs. I was black and looked younger than other senior NCOs. It really got their goat since I outranked them. SFC Muffet was the epitome of an old ignorant red neck. He never missed an opportunity to stab me in the back. I reminded him that promotions were not done by blood stripes. He never failed to feed the 1SG a bunch of crap about me. The 1SG lapped up Muffet's crap like a pig. Muffet informed the 1SG about me waking the privates up two minutes before lights on. The 1SG confronted me and said, "I hear you have been waking the privates up two minutes early." I answered, "By whose watch?" When I was not around, Muffet sabotaged my platoon.

He did it at a simulated grenade training exercise. We graded each other's platoon. The privates scored a Go or a No Go. I tried to be a team player. Ensured everyone in his platoon was effective enough to receive a Go. Upon completion of the exercise, I realized he failed almost every private in my platoon. He was degrading my privates to make me look bad. I could tell some of the privates were developing an inferiority complex, so I put them in a formation. While I had them at attention, I stated, "Sometimes people will do things to you to make you look bad. They figure by belittling others it makes them look good or feel big. There is one thing I want you to always remember: When you do your best or even exceed the standards of a task, you will always have haters. The best remedy for haters is to ignore them for, eventually, they will break themselves down by trying to degrade others. Therefore, keep your head up and do not let them see you sweat about meaningless stuff."

Not heeding my own words, finally, I had enough. I confronted the company commander about all of his backstabbing and his attitude toward my platoon. It was like talking to a brick wall. Her response was that "DI Muffet thinks like me." I simply stated, "That is a very scary thought." It was even scarier when Muffet was reduced in rank and lost his hat and patch. He demonstrated to a private, who had previously tried to commit suicide, how to actually complete the act. He took a razor to the private's throat to show where to cut the jugular vein. He also shaved the private's head with the razor.

After his demotion and release from the trail, some of the privates ordered pizza one night; and guess who delivered the pizza, it was Muffet dressed in a pizza boy outfit. Moreover, he ended up cheating them out of their change. You can bet that I got a real kick out of that story.

It was very obvious that Muffet's friend, the company commander, did not care too much for me. Regardless of that, I envied her dark, black mustache, and I was appalled at the boyish cut of her hair. Her bow legs and mannerism was a perfect match for her physical characteristics. I never liked speaking to her. Her breath smelt like she had just licked the last bit of d-o, d-o from a female's butt. My suspicion of Captain (CPT) Doggett was solidified when one of her girlfriends showed up to visit her for a few days. Both looked like something the cat dragged in, so it was difficult to tell who was screwing who.

Anyway, every chance the CPT got to make me look incompetent, she used it. She stayed in line with her similarities to Muffet because she eventually received a counseling statement for her antics. She really showed her true self during the female cycle.

Although difficult situations will arise with the male or female cycle, during the female cycle, a male DI must be extra careful to not place himself in a compromising situation. It does not call for a lot of hollering at sometimes. An incident occurred at a live night fire range, highlighting the point I am trying to make. I was a safety, manning two foxholes as live rounds were being fired down the range. I saw two females leave their foxhole very slowly and carefully. Immediately, I questioned them. I asked, "What is the problem?" They responded, "Drill Sergeant, something crawled into our foxhole. We think it is a snake." I waited until that round of firing was over before signaling for a cease-fire. The interruption allowed me to use a flashlight and inspect the foxhole. Sure enough, a rattler had crawled into their foxhole. I killed it with the butt of one of their rifles. I commended them for the manner in which they handled the situation. They did not panic and cause confusion during the live fire. It could have turned into a nightmare out there.

Times like the snake incident can happen on a daily basis, and it is imperative that the DI receives support in the performance of his duties. Again, I never felt comfortable with CPT Doggett as a company commander. Our bivouac is an ideal place and time to refer to. She and her recently appointed Peewee Herman-looking first sergeant stuck it to me and my platoon, consisting of about fifty females, as far back in the woods as they possibly could. They ensured that they placed all the other platoons right at the edge of the hill, particularly their buddy Muffet. All they had to do was walk down the hill to the command tent or mess area. I would have to walk more than fifty meters through thick forest.

That first night, I found myself stumbling around in the dark and drizzling rain, tightening tents. I did not want the girls' tents being blown down in the middle of the night and them waking up miserably soaked. Spending half the night cold and soaked at o'dark thirty in the morning, I had to get them ready to move from their sleeping positions to the mess area for breakfast. It took time for everyone to get ready, particularly in the dark. Finally, I verified the head count and made everyone grab hands. I led them through more than a hundred feet of woods and down a steep hill. Old "d-o d-o" breath really laid it on me when we were a few minutes late for breakfast. All other platoon sergeants smelt like roses. I knew I had not heard the end of it. She meant her verbal abuse as verbal counseling.

The bivouac ended in a thirteen-mile road march. During the march, privates and I were packed with more than fifty pounds of full rucksacks and weapons. We were in a tactical posture. I had to keep them at least five meters apart and have them march with caution. It still was a challenge to make everyone keep up. My assistant DI was responsible for stragglers and anyone experiencing medical problems. He had to ride on the ambulance to the aid station with one of the females, who was having physical problems. Believe me, I caught hell with all the complaining, crying, and lagging behind. From all the yelling, my voice became hoarse. Mentally, I was somewhat stressed. When I got back to the barracks, I needed a few minutes to myself before I assessed my platoon's physical condition. Moreover, I had to provide them with further instructions.

As soon as I arrived in my office, the CPT sent word for me to come down and see her. I told the messenger to tell her, "As soon as I check my platoon's injuries, feet, and mental stability, I will be there." The messenger delivered my message and returned, stating, "She said she wanted to see you now." I repeated the exact words I told the messenger the first time. She delivered it to her again. Obviously, the CPT did not like it, and she ran up into my office. In an upset tone, she shouted, "I thought I ordered you to report to me." I responded, "Do you know anything about the procedures after a road march? At this point and time, you should be more concerned about the condition of these privates. What is your problem?"

She returned to her office, and less than an hour later, I met with her. She was so anxious to see me so she could issue me a counseling statement for being late for breakfast on the bivouac. I wrote a two-page rebuttal, describing her attitude and behavior as a soldier and commander. The highlights of the rebuttal read as follows: "Throughout the past seven weeks, Captain Doggett's attitude and behavior does not emulate that of a Company Commander. Both are not conducive of one who is directly responsible for a company of basic trainees and drill instructors. She disregards the welfare of the trainees and some of the soldiers under her command. If she cared, I would not be forced to write this rebuttal. Instead, I would be upstairs checking the trainees' feet and ensuring none of them have ascertained any significant illnesses or injuries resulting from the 13-mile road march. We just finished the march a little more than an hour ago. Moreover, I had been waiting outside her office for half an hour. I am not surprised at her inappropriate mannerisms as company commander.

On numerous occasions, she has had privates standing for hours outside the building to be counseled by her. On bivouac, she displayed discrimination by placing my platoon and I in an unfavorable situation, knowing it would be difficult to meet time constraints. She placed her white buddy (DI Muffet) and his platoon at the edge of the hill. My platoon and I were grounded in a position as deep as possible in a thick, wooded area. She knew in hours of darkness it would be difficult to navigate. It was especially challenging early in the morning before daylight when we had to make it to breakfast. Punctuality was a necessity. We had time constraints to move out for the training of the day. Needless to say, we were a few minutes late and she was very nasty about it. As nasty as her disposition was in the field, I have seen her on several occasions display inappropriate behavior while in garrison.

I have witnessed her in the face of some of the female privates with a look of passion. Again, her conduct is unbecoming of a Commander. I am ashamed of being a soldier in her company. I request to be transferred to another company as soon as possible."

After I wrote my rebuttal, I took a minute to listen outside her office as I placed my ear close to her office door. She sounded as though she was in tears. Angrily, I heard her beckon, "1SG, take a look at what he wrote about me." Later that day, I was asked by the First Sergeant to drop the whole affair. I refused. "No, I will not drop it. Furthermore, I want her statement and mine to be sent to the battalion commander. Oh, and please see that the battalion command sergeant major receives a courtesy copy."

Another memorable incident involving her counseling me pertained to a female private. It began when a private was touched by a United States Army Reservist while at the dining facility. I reported it in my Charge of Quarters log, and I mentioned it to the CO when she walked through the barracks with me. Embarrassingly, when she came to the barracks and did not find me in the CQ area, she walked in the latrine right as I was urinating. My penis was in my hand. I did not think it was so small that she could not see it. She acted as if nothing was wrong. I suppose she was too busy trying to find something else to charge me with. There was no other reason for her to be there. The privates were in bed as we made our tour. I felt it was an ideal time to inform her of the incident at the dining facility. So I told her, "A server at the mess hall touched one of the privates." My explanation was interrupted when we noticed two privates in bed together. A private was consoling her battle buddy. She explained that her battle buddy received some bad news from home. Specifically, an aunt died. I made the one doing the consoling go back to her assigned bunk.

The next day, I could not believe that after telling her about the mess hall incident and reporting it in my Charge of Quarters log, CPT Doggett still wrote me up for not reporting it in a timely manner. I knew I was in Alabama, but give me a break. This is an officer in the United States Army and the year is 1989. Again, a DI has too many other concerns than to be bothered with continued harassment against him.

Michael Conrad

One of the most cynical things that occurred involved the doings of a male private while I was on the trail. He enlisted as Michael I. Conrad. Standing about five feet ten, he was plump bellied with red hair and green eyes. A bit older than the typical recruit, I could see how his peers probably looked at him as an older brother.

So upon his arrival to boot camp, it did not take him long to establish rapport with his fellow trainees. He gained the confidence of the privates within his group to the point that he became their mail handler. Although I was the DI for the fourth platoon, at times, I would have an acquired responsibility for the entire company. Times such as physical training, formations, chow, and various types of training afforded the DIs to get acquainted with trainees in other platoons.

One evening, it was my turn to control the company for chow. Usually, I look privates up and down. I happened to place myself in a position to maintain eye-to-eye contact with Michael. He responded in an introvert manner, but he mustered a half smile from under his cap. As I walked closer to him with a serious demeanor, I said, "You have the look of someone very untrustworthy. For some reason, I do not trust you." I have no idea why those words came out of my mouth. I never knew he was the mail handler for his platoon. My statements turned out to be very accurate. The truth began to unravel a few weeks later. DI James from third platoon thought he saw someone who looked like PVT Conrad at a bus terminal. Later, he explained, "I did not think anything of it because I figured it was someone else who looked like him." The morning after DI James saw the person, PVT Conrad was missing from the PT formation. After searching the barracks, it was determined that he was AWOL.

The investigation for PVT Conrad opened a Pandora's Box. In the first place, he was not Michael Conrad, he was Thomas Conrad. He faked his identity by using his brother's social security number to enter the Army. Moreover, he was wanted by the Federal Bureau of Investigations and local law enforcement authorities in the Des Moines, Iowa area. Now the army is on his trail for going AWOL, and to add to it, he stole valuable items from the privates. Many of the privates were concerned why no one was receiving their mail. Their mail included other items besides letters. Monetary notes, money orders, gift cards, and other valuables were among the many items. The articles must have totaled up to thousands of dollars. My question to the recruiters was, "How did you allow someone to enlist in the United States Army under false pretenses without someone catching it during the process. Were you so pressured by Desert Storm that you enlisted as many bodies as possible without thoroughly screening them? Did you ever think about the welfare of the naïve and innocent privates?"

Speaking about the welfare of naïve and innocent privates, a miscue almost developed as I was in charge of a One Station Unit Training Unit (OSUT). Our company was in charge of a chemical decontamination training exercise. Out of all the senior NCOs with a military occupational specialty (MOS) in chemicals, the company commander selected me. Initially, I tried to convince him, "Why don't you use a chemical NCO? I am in the medical field." Quickly, he snapped, "Them dumb sons of bitches. I do not trust them." I questioned, "Why did they get promoted if they do not know their job? Give them a chance." I sparred with him back and forth. Judging from some of his comments, he must have known about my tours as an infantryman/cavalry scout. He must have previewed my 201 files (personal records).

Was that the basis for his decision? My intent was to give him a hard time before I accepted the responsibility. Besides, he was my company commander and a good friend.

Our mission was to set-up a chemical decontamination station. We had to perform decontamination on tactical vehicles such as five and two-and-a-half-ton trucks. On the day of the exercise, the early morning temperature was already above 100 degrees Fahrenheit in the shade. The heat along with our Military Oriented Protective Posture (MOPP) gear we had to wear over our battle dress uniform was a recipe for heat casualties. The M17 protective mask added to that vulnerability. Therefore, the privates' welfare was paramount.

My first order of business was a formation for accountability of personnel, uniforms, and equipment. I was in charge of a platoon size element. A total of fifty privates were reported present or accounted for in a secluded tract of wooded land infested with snakes, mosquitoes, various other creatures, and pests. Everyone was placed in their appropriate security positions approximately ten meters apart, and all components of the decontamination process were sequentially spread further apart in accordance with the field manual. The dynamics of the exercise meshed outstandingly. After about a couple of hours, the commander signaled "all clear" to remove protective masks. We concluded the exercise in the late afternoon. I held another formation for accountability. This time, the count was forty-nine privates. I asked the squad leaders to verify the count. The count of forty-nine was still reported. Without hesitation, I put everyone on line at double arm interval to scour the woods in search of the missing private. Five minutes later, we found him face down with his protective mask still on. I shook him to get a response and found him to be conscious. Then I removed his mask, gave him water, and loosened his clothes. Once he appeared revived, I asked him, "What happened, private? Did you hear the all clear?" Drowsily, he blurted, "No, drill sergeant." I snapped, "Did you fall asleep?" Confused, he stated, "No, drill sergeant." Although I had my own suspicion about what happened to him, I directed one of the NCOs to take him to the hospital. It was better to be safe than sorry. Relieved that we found him, I knew we could have easily conceded that we miscounted from the morning formation or someone left without being reported. I felt fortunate about demanding a search because the private could have died out. The incident involving the missing private during the decontamination exercise brings to mind the female private I almost lost.

WILL POWER

It was late in the cycle. Only one private in my platoon did not meet the minimum requirement of passing the Army Physical Fitness Readiness Test (APFRT). Etta May Jones from Mississippi was the opposite of Cover Girl and definitely was not among the brightest stars in the universe. With low self-esteem, her hair was short and filled with knaps. Gingivitis did not make for a pleasant conversation with her. I was disturbed by her lack of motivation. In the midst of about three push-ups, she crashed her short, overweight body to her knees; therefore, she also lacked willpower. Moreover, she was a high school dropout. I decided to work with her one-on-one to see her succeed in something.

"How do I increase her willpower?" was the first question I asked my assistant platoon sergeant. The second question was, "How do you motivate someone who has not passed any pertinent challenges in life?"

Nonetheless, I took it as a challenge to help her accomplish something in her life. I had always taken pride in motivating and conditioning everyone in the platoon to exceed the Army Physical Fitness Readiness Test (APFRT). Because of my rigid methods of physical conditioning, I was nicknamed the Prince of Pump. When I told the privates to pump, they knew to start doing push-ups. As they conducted their repetitions, I had them say, "Drill SGT, thank you for conditioning my mind and my body to help me understand the principle of pump. Feel free to do so at any time." I would say, "I will." After completion of the required repetitions, they requested permission to recover. My mentality was that failure was not an option. I did not want PVT Jones to fail.

My brief to the brigade commander (BCDR) of PVT Jones's status was very optimistic. When he asked if I felt she could pass, I responded, "I am going to motivate her and do more anaerobic exercises with her. With a little one on one, I see no reason why she cannot pass the test." The briefing was interrupted with a knock on the conference room door as I spoke. It was my assistant platoon sergeant, DI Baker. He waved me to the door. I told him to hold on as I was briefing the BCDR. He said that it was very important. The BCDR told me to go ahead. DI Baker exclaimed, "PVT Jones just tried to kill herself!" He went on to say, "She slit her wrist and stuck her head in the gas oven." I told him, "Get her to the hospital." Reluctantly, I informed the BCDR, "Disregard last transmission. Private Jones just attempted suicide." He excused me to go and see her.

It took a while for me to get over it. I tried to rationalize what happened. Was she so full of shame that she attempted suicide because all of her peers had succeeded in passing the AFRT? Did she decide at that moment to give up on life because of all her shortcomings? Besides not graduating from high school, she had personal issues that I felt she was not mature enough to take care of. Personal issues such losing weight, staying well-groomed, and focusing on her short-term and long-term goals were the items I discussed with her. I tried to relay the importance of not giving up in basic training and how she would benefit from it. Succeeding in basic training could open new doors.

Then I began to wonder if she used the Army policy on the attempt to commit suicide. The policy at the time mandated automatic separation procedures on any trainee attempting suicide. After I calmed down, I asked myself, "Whose life is it anyway?" Besides, it is not my life. As much as I wanted her to succeed, I cannot will a person to succeed. He or she has to have some self-motivation and self-esteem of their own. On the brighter side of things, it was gratifying to reflect on the fact that all the other females had succeeded and moved on to the next stage of training or careers. They had withstood all the early cold mornings of the rifle ranges, physical training, the thirteen-mile road march, common task testing, and all the strenuous mental and physical situations they had encountered during the past eight weeks of basic training.

Every now and then, I run into one of my former privates or soldiers, and I get a handshake. Many have grown to become successful commissioned officers, noncommissioned officers, or accomplished civilians. One day, as I lowered the chair in my operatory with an army major occupying it, she looked up at me and said, "I know you." Bewildered, I stated, "You do?" She was so excited, saying, "You were my DI in basic training. This is so cool. I cannot wait to get home and tell my husband and my mom. You are the reason I did not give up and continued my military career." I treated her on another occasion. I had a chance to hear her story of how her husband and her mother reacted. It felt good to have someone excited about seeing me again. It happened another time with a male soldier almost under the same circumstances and wearing the rank of a major as well. He remembered me as saying very little. But when I did speak, everyone knew to listen or face tiresome consequences.

As I go on with my life, I continue to run into former privates and soldiers. All the handshakes and thanks I receive give me a wonderful feeling of gratification. That is what makes life worth living.

HARD HEAD CITY

Army Instructor

Upon making a left onto Saratoga Street from Martin Luther King Avenue, the activities of street life and the public housing areas were extremely busy. The older heads were playing checkers, dominos, or cards. The look and smell of cigarette or marijuana smoke polluted the air. Everyone seemed to be holding a forty. The pushers had the look to say, "I got what you need." The crack-heads were leaning so low to the ground that it would make someone ask the questions, "Why don't they fall? and What is holding them up?" Trash cluttered the streets. I saw a ran-over dead rat in the middle of the road. He was as big as a guinea pig. Smack dab in the midst of this section 8 area stood the high school, my ultimate destination near downtown Baltimore. There I was, headed for an interview with the principal; I did not have the slightest idea what I was getting into. Although I had been in and out of the city on several occasions, I paid more attention to details during this drive.

For anyone not familiar with the area, Baltimore is a seaport city located approximately forty miles north of Washington DC. It sits at the tidal portion of the Patapsco River and at head of the Chesapeake Bay. As with many national and international port cities, it breeds a vast and diverse array of crimes. Drugs are among the most prevalent. In addition, the city is at the top of the list in the rate of sexually transmitted diseases per capita. Taking all things into consideration, I was offered an army instructor position there at an alternative high school in July of 1993.

The Interview

A sign in front of an antiquated building displayed the institution's name. The first thing I noticed was bullets holes in the front door. It is a very scary sight, particularly if the front door is attached to an educational institution that serves hundreds of children. I made my way up the steps. Later, for obvious reasons, I came to refer to the school as Hard Head City (HHC) because the real name would not imply its hostile atmosphere and surroundings. A poor hand-written paper note provided me with instructions to ring the buzzer for entrance into the building. Sticking out like a disoriented boy at a girl's preparatory school, I was nothing but spit and polish, all decked out in my army class A uniform. The uniform represented my full array of ribbons and decorations accomplished during my twenty-two years of military service. I was definitely dressed to impress for my career-changing interview.

Finding my way to the main office area, the first person I saw was the principal's secretary, Ms. Hughes. How she squeezed into that little chair without it breaking to pieces bewildered me. I quickly realized that she had the attitude of a predatory pit bull. The elephant collars of the red dress were trimmed in black, and the red, pointed-toe, high-heeled shoes were a perfect match. Believe it or not, she even wore red-colored panty hose. Nonetheless, I could not stand the smell of her eau de toilette. "Can I help you?" was the very first words she uttered. She never looked up. I replied, "I am 1SG Melvin Heard. I have an interview with Dr. Bobby Barfield." Deliberately, she nodded, "I will let him know you are here."

It was about five minutes before I was escorted to the principal's office by Ms. Vivian Austin. She was the assistant principal. She introduced me to Dr. Barfield. He conducted an impromptu head-to-toe inspection of me as I took a seat. In stature, he reminded me of Barney Rubble. He began sharing his plans with me. His vision was to create a Junior Reserve Officer Training Corps Battalion at HHC. He explained that HHC was an alternative school. In other words, it was one of few schools in the city that allowed Baltimore City High School students to graduate at a faster pace. The school year was based on trimesters instead of semesters. A student could earn three credits a trimester, which meant nine credits a year instead of six with two semesters. Twenty-one credits were required to graduate. From his briefing, I gathered that the character of the student population warranted a unique strategy.

After providing me with the history of the school, he asked me to share a little bit about myself. I informed him that, initially, I began my career as an infantryman/scout reclassified to the dental field and spent two years as a drill sergeant. I felt the drill instructor duty was very important relative to the position of an AI. It provided me with the insight of training cadets as I had trained male and female trainees or soldiers.

The Ajrotc Program

Eventually, I was hired to be an army instructor. At the same time, Major William "Rusty" Cobb was brought aboard as the senior army instructor (SAI). He was a relatively short man of medium build and with gray hair. He displayed more of a pessimistic attitude that helped to offset my optimistic and aggressive nature. We pretty much complemented each other.

On the first day of school, my anxiety was as high as a young bull's debut in a corral with all heifers. My years as an army drill instructor taught me that first impressions were very important. However, it did not take long to find out just what I had to deal with. To my despair, the homeroom class straggled in nonchalantly. Almost everyone was late. When they did show up, most were unprepared. Some even had the nerve to bring chicken baskets to the classroom. Without permission, they wanted to sit there and eat right in front of my face. I did not appreciate that. Furthermore, the guys were calling the girls Bs, and the girls calling the guys MFs. Later, I realized many of the students were crack babies. Their manners were worse than baby pigs playing musical chairs while sharing their mother's breast. Immediately, I had to restore order and establish my turf.

Beforehand, I had written my rules for the classroom. I read the following to them:

1. Be on time
2. Be prepared for class
3. Show respect for others
4. Raise your hand and ask permission to speak
5. No cursing
6. Complete all homework assignments
7. Participate in class
8. Conduct yourselves as cadets
9. Act as assistant instructors for other teachers
10. Wear your uniform on the designated days

Judging by their expressions and attitudes, they cared less about rules. Most had never been held accountable for any guidelines. The majority of the young ladies had a child or two already. A lot of the young men were involved with drugs, carjacking, or other crimes. They had done these things before reaching the ninth grade.

At least for the first week, the classes were almost full. In the weeks to come, students began to drop off. Some dwindled in and out. If five of them showed up for class at any given period, it constituted a record. The SAI and I tried to come up with methods to keep them involved in our program as well as the school. We sponsored leadership weekends and raised funds to send cadets to summer camp.

Leadership weekends ran from Friday night until Sunday. Usually, we conducted them with a county school. My intentions were for the inner city kids to learn from the county kids and vice versa. The shock treatment was implemented on the first night with uniform, barracks, and wall locker inspection.

Being a First Sergeant (1SG) and the highest ranking noncommissioned officer, usually, I was in charge of the inspection. All former drill instructors (DIs), me included, wore our round brown hats. The hat was a key factor in gaining intimidation. Surely, it was an advantage we needed in controlling hundreds of cadets. Mentally, I wanted to subject them to as much fear as I could. Daily, in the classroom, I faced their belligerent and nasty attitudes. Discipline and teamwork were my goals. I would think of legal DI tactics to make life as uncomfortable for them as I could. At the same time, I wanted to remind them of how the teachers felt when they went on their temper tantrums or displayed negative behaviors in the classroom.

The inspection was a tool that forced discipline and teamwork. Preparing for it required a high degree of coordination. The tactic of "front loading" was used for the start time of the inspection. Front loading meant imposing a time limit on an event, knowing the task would not be efficiently and sufficiently accomplished on time. The purpose was for them to work as a team and minimize the amount of "gigs" (demerits). For instance, if they worked as a team to make their bunks, clean the barracks, and work on their uniforms, they would accomplish more. But no, they spent most of their time arguing with each other, especially the ones we intentionally put together as battle buddies. Despite not liking each, we wanted them to overcome that challenge and accomplish something together.

On one particular weekend, I knew the battle buddy of Devin Harris from HHC caught hell. Devin's feet smelt so bad that he had the entire barracks smelling worse than skunk squirt. I almost condemned the barracks. And on another weekend, this one female neglected to bring toilet articles not to mention sanitation napkins. We had to purchase everything for her. It appeared as though she had not bathed for weeks. Some of the other female cadets testified that when she took a shower, they could see the dirty water run down the drain.

On another memorable occasion, I twisted the rules by letting twelve elementary school kids join us for the weekend. They were students who constantly gave teachers in Baltimore City a hard time. My intentions were to scare them and have them experience something that they would never forget. I threatened them up front about their behavior and why they were here. My exact words were, "When I finish with you this weekend, I better not hear about you giving any teacher a hard time. If you do, I will come down to the school, bite your little balls off, chew them up, and spit them dead in your face." Honestly, I must admit that they displayed a high degree of stamina and tenacity aside from a couple of them urinating in their bunks.

Getting back to the point about the inspections, it never surprised me that by the time we inspected their uniforms and barracks, the cadets' mental and physical capacities were in disarray. Their uniforms were a disgrace, and most could not answer questions that they knew answers to without stuttering or breaking out in tears. I reminded them of how tough they were when torturing the teachers in their classroom. I emphasized the fact that the teachers were trying to educate their dumb butts. In the meantime, throughout the inspection, my assistant inspectors and I flipped bunks, threw clothing and other items out of their assigned wall lockers. I had someone place cooked liver in the toilet to give the illusion of stool in the toilet. At the end of the inspection, I beckoned everyone to the latrine. My very words were: "I cannot believe during my inspection that someone pooped in my toilet and did not flush it." At that moment, I reached in the toilet, grabbed the liver, let it run down through my fingers, down my arm, and flung it to the floor. All the cadets jumped back, except one little female cadet. Sneaking through the crowd she stated, "1SG, I think it was me." The other instructors and I practically bit our lips to keep from laughing. We kept our composure, and in an angry manner, we made them get down and do about one hundred push-ups. When the push-ups were over, I asked, "Is everybody mad?" They answered, "Yes." Then I would say, "Excellent. Now, together, you all have something mutually exclusive. Everybody is mad at me, and that's the beginning of a team. It is a small beginning but nonetheless a beginning." I then warned them of the consequences of failing the re-inspection in the morning.

Although we tried to make life miserable for the cadets on leadership weekend cadets, they had a lot of fun and fringe benefits. Many took advantage of washing bags of filthy clothes for free. The mess hall served a variety of foods. They ate well and as much as they wanted. Training in first aid, physical fitness, geography, teamwork, drill and ceremonies, and other topics were provided. We even ran them through confidence courses and land navigation courses. The confidence courses were designed to promote teamwork while the land navigation courses helped them become proficient in reading a map and using a lensatic compass. They earned liberty based on the results of the inspections and training. Additionally, attitude and behavior played roles in our decision. Their liberty time entailed going to the post-exchange, bowling alley, movies, go-kart riding, and other events. By the end of the weekend, one could sense the attitude changes by many of the cadets. Those nasty personalities seemed to magically disappear and were replaced by courtesy, respect, and discipline, along with a show of teamwork.

INDEPENDENCE CARDS

Generally, the student population at HHC lacked proper parental guidance. *En otras palabras*, they did not have table manners or home training. The expression of a caring attitude among peers was a sign of weakness in their eyes. Their mannerism displayed toughness and argumentative confrontations. Their goals were based on generations of behavior, primarily inherited from their parents.

The term "crack babies" were used to describe some of the children displaying irrational behavior. The ideology was that their mothers were on crack during the time of pregnancy. Needless to say, they lacked classroom etiquette. They were incoherent and had a recognizable psychedelic frame of mind. Most could not complete a sentence without the use of profanity, and often enough they would misconstrue the content of an on-going discussion. Again and again, this would lead to argument after argument and threats. On a daily basis, I would be confronted by verbal attacks or would have an unpleasant conversation with someone. Gradually, I gained confidence from many students. Utilizing a little tact helped me communicate with them without always conforming to their wants or say things they wanted to hear. Most began to realize my intentions were for their best interest. I still had my haters because I did not sugar coat my words. Some of the females had me puzzled from the lack of not establishing higher goals.

MOTHER'S DAY

Many of the females did not aspire of becoming prosperous or living above the gains provided by public assistance. They were content on having a baby or two just to qualify for welfare. The benefits included public housing and the receipt of an independence card. Their attitudes were modeled from generations. Incidences of underage teen students still living with their parents at home sleeping with older men were not uncommon. The parents lived in public housing. As I understood it, credits for independence cards were made available at the end of the month in lieu of welfare checks. The day they were given the spending power was called "Mother's Day."

In 1999, the hip-hop group Bone Thugs-n-Harmony created their hit tune the *1st of tha Month*. The tune depicts a scenario that provides the listening audience an utmost colorful audio version of happenings when the welfare checks arrive.

Nonetheless, I was very surprised by the many ways the card could be used, either legally or illegally. Many cardholders worked deals. They secured cash by letting a non-cardholder use the independence card to purchase a certain amount of food. The going rate was receiving 50 percent cash money of the purchase price of food or other items. Those cards were a major source of living to many Baltimore residents. Therefore, the city government began to tie ineligibility for government assistance with school attendance.

Karen Hunt

For the most part, the attitude and behavior of the female student population at HHC reminded me of a chameleon. One never knew from one moment to another their true colors. Explicitly, they cursed, initiated arguments with the boys, and constantly wanted to fight each other. Disturbingly, I had to scold one for feeling me on my "behind." Daily, other faculty members and I stood outside the building in order to prevent fights after school. The females were notorious for fighting. On one occasion, after I overheard one of my students muttering the words: "Look at her. Why is she looking at me? She better stop looking at me," I warned her not to start a fight. I might as well have been talking to a deranged and mad Doberman Pinscher. I had not turned my back a minute before she walked across the street and snatched the other girl's extensions from her hair. Both girls ended up expelled.

There were a few atypical female students I tried to mentor. One student in particular would always speak to me personally concerning an array of topics. Her café au lait skin tone, her light dreamy green eyes, her slightly bow legs, along with her almost perfect 10 figure made Karen Hunt a remarkably attractive young lady. The only unnatural blemish was the streaks of brown and slightly gold colors of her hair. She was blessed with natural beauty. My definition of beauty is not just by physical characteristics but by personality and attitude as well. Her attitude and personality are nowhere near the arrogance displayed by many of the other female students. For the most part, she was well mannered and caring. Besides, she did not have a child or two like many of the others. I wanted all of them to succeed in their future endeavors and become prosperous, but she was willing and readily able. We spoke on a variety of topics, from her having a relationship with a young man to planning her career. The first thing I wanted her to enforce was to never let anyone disrespect her as a young lady.

I outlined her short-term and long-term goals. My primary concern at the time was for her to complete high school and not to be stymied by being "hot for boys." I kept hinting on the fact that a Reserve Officer Training Corps scholarship required a grade point average of 2.5 and a SAT score of 920. If she did not want to go that route, I advised her to take advantage of everything she would accomplishment from the Army Junior Reserve Training Officer Corps (AJROTC) program to document her college applications.

Karen stayed focused for months until she failed to be present at school for a couple of weeks. I tried contacting her, but all my attempts ended in failure. Then one day, I received a letter at the school with a return address from a Baltimore City jail. It read as follows:

Dear First Sergeant,

I know you were probably worried about me. It took some time for me to force myself to write you this letter. I want to thank you for taking the time and effort to mentor me. You have been a great mentor and friend. First, I must tell you that I am sorry for what I have done. Please, understand I had no choice. My boyfriend and I had an argument. He started to beat me. He kept beating and beating and beating me. I grabbed the first thing that I could get my hands on. That was a butcher knife. I stabbed him in his heart but he kept on trying to beat me. Eventually, I stabbed him to death, although it took a while for him to die. I did not know that he was on crack throughout our relationship. Hopefully, I will get out on self-defense. Keep me in your prayers and please forgive me for what I have done. I say again, I had no choice.

A Friend Always
Karen Hunt

She also left a mailing address. Friends and faculty collected money to help her with the lawyer's fees. Because of a job change, I went to another school, therefore, I never knew the outcome of her trial. However, my feelings were expressed in writing the following poem.

Karen Hunt

Karen Hunt, Karen Hunt,
Karen Hunt, Karen Hunt,
Just a sweet inner-city
girl,
Karen Hunt,
who grew up in a cold
and bitter world.
Karen Hunt,
she never got hi'.
Karen Hunt,
she never got drunk.
Karen Hunt,
all she wanted was an
Education,
Karen Hunt,
and a chance to be an
asset to our nation.

Karen Hunt, Karen Hunt,
after several days
passed,
Karen Hunt,
I was concerned for she
wasn't in class.
Karen Hunt,
I received her letter
from a B'more jail.
Karen Hunt,
she said, " presently,
my life is a living hell".

Karen Hunt, Karen Hunt,
Just a sweet inner-city
girl,
Karen Hunt,
who grew up in a cold
and bitter world.
Karen Hunt,
she never got hi'.
Karen Hunt,

she never got drunk.
Karen Hunt,
all she wanted was an
education,
Karen Hunt,
and a chance to be an
asset to our nation.

Karen Hunt, Karen Hunt,
she confided in me with
her problems.
Karen Hunt,
I did my best to help
her solve them.

But, then came an
incident,
Karen Hunt,
and it was too late.
Karen Hunt,
a knife through the
heart
sealed her boyfriend's
fate.
Karen Hunt,
she stated in the letter
that she had no choice.
Karen Hunt,
I could just imagine the
sound of her voice.

Karen Hunt, Karen Hunt,
Just a sweet inner-city
girl,
Karen Hunt,
who grew up in a cold
and bitter world.
Karen Hunt,
she never got hi'.
Karen Hunt,
she never got drunk
Karen Hunt,

all she wanted was an
education,
Karen Hunt,
and a chance to be an
asset to our nation.

Karen Hunt, Karen Hunt,
Just a sweet inner-city
girl,
Karen Hunt,
who grew up in a cold
and bitter world.
Karen Hunt,
she never got hi'.
Karen Hunt,
she never got drunk
Karen Hunt,
all she wanted was an
education,
Karen Hunt,
and a chance to be an
asset to our nation.

Karen Hunt, Karen Hunt,
"lumps and bruises",
Karen Hunt,
"were all over my face".
Karen Hunt,
"I tried to run,
Karen Hunt,
but he kept with the
chase".
Karen Hunt,
"I grabbed the first
object",
Karen Hunt,
"within my reach".
Karen Hunt,
"and now I'm strapped
down
like a dog on a leach".

Karen Hunt, Karen Hunt,
Just a sweet inner-city
girl,
Karen Hunt,
who grew up in a cold
and bitter world.
Karen Hunt,
she never got hi'.
Karen Hunt,
she never got drunk
Karen Hunt,
all she wanted was an
education,
Karen Hunt,
and a chance to be an
asset to our nation.

Karen Hunt, Karen Hunt,
"I did not know",
Karen Hunt,
"he was on crack or
cocaine".
Karen Hunt,
"until I saw the needle
marks in his veins".

Karen Hunt, Karen Hunt,
Just a sweet inner-city
girl,
Karen Hunt,
who grew up in a cold
and bitter world.
Karen Hunt,
she never got hi'.
Karen Hunt,
she never got drunk
Karen Hunt,
all she wanted was an
education,
Karen Hunt,
and a chance to be an
asset to our nation.

CALVIN KERR, JR.

Jonathan Smith

From my experiences with my cadets and students at HHC, I felt for the most part that they were not so bad. Yet, the males, as well as the females, had their own personal issues. Collectively, my assessment of their problems stemmed from a lack of guidance and discipline at home. Some were lost, and it was very obvious that no one had taken the time to monitor their activities.

One day, I had a visit from an investigative reporter from the *Baltimore Sun*. He came to question me about Jonathan Smith, a young black man. Jonathan stood about six feet tall and slender. He was light skinned with a very quiet disposition.

The writer was trying to find out the last day Jonathan attended school. Judging from my attendance records, Jonathan had not shown up to school in about four weeks. At that point in my life, I realized the importance of accurately keeping attendance records.

During the conversation with the reporter, he informed me of the following incidences. He stated that about four weeks ago, Jonathan was invited to a party by an adult black man. The invitee had just recently been released from a New York City prison. He had served a sentenced for a sexually related incident. Therefore, the man is a suspect in this case which involves the rape and murder of Jonathan Smith.

The aforementioned incidences bring to mind many questions when it comes to our children. "How many Jonathan Smiths are there?" "How many Karen Hunts are there?" "How can we resolve the neglect of hundreds and thousands of our children?" "What sort of institution can we devise to motivate education and training that would be conducive to our children needs?" Think for a moment of the numerous cities that encounter all the fatal, tragic and bitter situations around and upon the grounds of their educational institutions described in this story. Keep in mind that Hard Head City is not a label for just the cities themselves, it refers to the mental, physical, and environmental culture of their institutions as well.

Remember The Pirates

Well before my military career began, I have always had an interest in sports, particularly basketball. The necessity of working part-time ended my brief stint as a player in high school. After I joined the army, I was in the best condition of my life. I participated in all my unit's basketball, flag football, and softball games. Whatever sport I played, I took pride in winning. Usually, we did just that.

Throughout my whole life, coaching basketball was one of my utmost desires. After being hired as an Army Instructor HHC, it did not take very long for me to become an assistant to the head basketball coach for the HHC Pirates. The head coach, Mr. Edwin Dawkins, provided me the opportunity to coach basketball at the high school level.

Eventually, I became the head coach. Previously, the extent of my basketball coaching included a dual role. While in the army, I was a player-coach for my unit's basketball team on many occasions. On two of those occasions, we won league championships. At HHC, I knew the challenge would be a little bit different. Instead of dealing with men, I had to manage hard-headed teenagers. Conditioning was my primary focus. Secondly, I always delivered a suggested offensive and defensive plan before the game.

Both schemes were run as a reflection of my character and attitude when it came to competition. My attack mode was attributed to my army background that consisted of some of the following jobs: infantryman, grenadier, M60 machine gunner, infantry scout, and drill instructor. Those were just a few jobs to paint a gross picture of my career and for one to understand my mentality when it comes to physical fitness.

Everyone had to be in excellent condition. Before we worked on any plays, the players had to run a mile or two. The run was followed by a series of calisthenics consisting of the following:

- multiple stretching exercises
- push-ups
- sit-ups
- duck walks
- jogging in place
- lateral and backward movements
- line touches
- figure eights

Other methods of training were used as I deemed necessary to adjust the team's attitude. Initially, many of the players were reluctant to participate in the grueling methods of conditioning. However, I would always respond by telling them to quit. My responses were, "Quit! Quit! Quit! We do not need you. I know you have probably been smoking that crack and drinking that gin and juice. I am going to run it out of you. I do not want junkies on the team, and I certainly do not want quitters. You might have a withdrawal or probably quit on us while the game is in progress. Do us a favor and not waste our time. Quit!" Many of them would defy my inferences with replies of their own while moaning and groaning.

In practice, I refereed the scrimmages. I selected the squads and had them play games without dribbling. Dribbling was a turnover. At the end of practice, if they did not make seven out of ten shots from the free throw line, they had to run five more laps around the basketball court. My boot camp-like practices were intended to make the players sweat a lot and eliminate whatever toxins they put in their bodies. On one occasion, while giving a player a ride, he pointed to a policeman in a car alongside me. He insinuated that the policeman probably wanted some crack because he had sold him some in the past. I did not know whether to believe him or not. However, I never took chances on the condition of my players, for I have imagined their inner-city lifestyles.

NIQUE

Often times, I would allow scrimmages with the neighborhood gang. I felt it would promote a positive community relationship. My idea backfired as tensions from the games spilled out onto the streets. The neighborhood became a hostile environment for the team, the Army JROTC cadets, and other students. There were instances of students being badly beaten. I sometimes wonder if the death of Nique was in direct correlation to the conflict between the school and community. One never knows what causes shootings such as this.

Dominique Sherman was also in a special program. He had a short attention span and a quick temper. This may have had something to do with his death. I, at one time, had to break up a fight between him and one of the gang members. It appeared to me that their disagreement did not start there but from a past altercation. They were already acquainted with each other. I could see the dislike for each other in their eyes. After I brought them together for a handshake, I had a feeling the dispute was not over.

I received the call about Nique's death from one of the JROTC instructors. Sergeant Robert Hutchison (Bobby) informed me that Nique had been shot about ten times. According to Bobby, as I called him, Nique's mother wanted me to attend the funeral.

I thought back to a game when I was confronted by his mother because I did not allow Nique to play but for a few minutes. His mother gave me the impression that she and Nique rolled like sisters and brothers rather than mother and son. She did not understand why I would not let him play because he could not stay focused. He was more about the hype than he was about the team winning. Besides, he tried everything he could to get out of practice. He would try to hide during the one or two mile run. He went to the bathroom during calisthenics. When I did let him play, he seemed as though he only wanted to play offense because his man would be on one side of the court, and he would be at the opposite side. After the confrontation with his mother, he never showed up for practice or any games. The team went on to complete an unblemished season.

15-0

My thoughts are that at any level with any sport, a coach and his team has to be skilled and fortunate to survive a season undefeated. In one game, for instance, we were down by twelve points with less than two minutes to go. My strategy was to extend the game by filing, using full-court pressured defense and shooting three-point shots. The pressured defense led to turnovers. The turnovers led to fast breaks resulting in lay ups. When the fast breaks were not there, I demanded them from our three-point sharpshooter. The sharpshooter was instructed to always trail the play. To our fortunes, we found ourselves in control of the basketball with thirteen seconds left to play in the game. With my last time out, I set the play. The first words out of my mouth were, "Do not turn the ball over. I can live with missing a shot rather than having a turnover. All players receiving a pass must move toward the ball." My point guard was like an assistant coach on the floor; therefore, he received special instructions for the play. I trusted him to make a play, so I told him, "You must have the ball in your hands at five seconds to make your move to the goal. Five seconds will give us time enough for a tip in just in case we miss. Your first is to try to blow pass your man at the top of the key. Try to take it all the way to the hoop. If your defender gets help from a big man, dump off to a forward. Both will delay and come from the wings. They will be in position for a pass or a rebound/tip-in." Tarik did not need to dump off. When he blew by his defender, no one came over. As he scored the basket, the clock ran out.

With that season and all of my other seasons, I never cut anyone. Players like Nique cut themselves. They did not need my help. One sure way was not coming to school and getting expelled by the eighteen-day rule. Maintaining at least a C grade point average or not passing more than half of their classes cut many as soon as the first report cards came out. Additionally, if they were not in school the day of the game, they could not play. Moreover, they could not have reached their nineteenth birthday before the start of the basketball season. Sometimes putting five legitimate players on the court was a challenge in itself. That was a far few than the over forty on the first day of practice.

Despite all of the different challenges taking place in the course of a season, we would win either the regular season championship or the tournament, and sometimes both. It was my last season when we went undefeated. I believe I worked harder than any time in my life. I was always extremely fatigued when I lay down at night. Between instructing, coaching, and parenting, I did not have much me time. Therefore, every minute of practice with the basketball team was highly valuable. Aerobically, I used a two mile run to start practice. My anaerobic drills consisted of push-ups and sit-ups. Taking them to muscle failure was my ultimate goal before the figure eights. Discussing, demonstrating, and walking through defensive strategies came before offensive plays.

The 3-1-1 full court or straight man-to-man defenses were always my favorites. The concept of the 3-1-1 is to apply pressure on the ball without playing a man-to-man. On made baskets, the 3-1-1 was applied and a man-to-man off of misses. Every starter and bench player must know his position when the 3-1-1 is implemented. It required a vast amount of stamina; therefore, fresh players must be ready to enter the game at all times. Sagging shorts immediately eliminated you from entering the game. Not knowing your position on defense or not playing your man on defense took you out. After defensive strategies, we worked on offensive and situational plays. Most of our offense was created by the defense.

The defense created the two-on-one, three-on-one, etc. advantages we looked for. The two offensive plays were dictated to us from the opponent's defense. One was to counter a man-to-man and the other to disrupt a zone. Situational plays consisted of breaking and scoring off the press, scoring from out of bound plays, taking time off the clock, and taking the last shot.

The rewards of the time I spent drilling the team on taking time off the clock, taking the last shot, and shooting free throws eventually paid off in the last high school championship game. Champions of the Walter G. Amprey League, superintendent of the school board in Baltimore City, winning the championship game would also ensure a perfect season. We were the number 1 seed, and I had no problem with the game being played on a neutral site. My problem was with the opponent's roster. The opposing coaches put "ringers" in their line-up. There were at least three players I had not seen on their roster all season. We had played them and beat them three times already. For this game, I saw players six feet seven, six feet eight, and six feet nine all of a sudden eligible to play basketball. Obviously, I could not hold back my anger. I was so upset that I called the other coaches out. My first words to them were, "You could not beat us legally, so you go out and recruit ringers. I personally would take either one of you one-on-one with a referee, of course. And as old as I am, I will beat you. Being a coach constitutes more than wearing the title. You have to understand the rules of the game and skill levels of all your players. Moreover, their physical stamina and endurance play a major part in winning and losing. That is where we will beat you. We will run the ball down your throats." The last thing I told my team before going on the floor was, "Run the ball down their throat and make them foul you. Make the referee have to call something."

My starting line-up consisted of the following players:

At point guard—Tarik "Trickie" Downs is six feet two inches tall, and he had mad ball-handling skills. He was the floor general, and he was like my assistant coach on the floor. At the end of the game, he was the one guy that I trusted with the ball in his hands when it came to the last shot. I knew that he would make the right decision, creating his own shot or a shot for someone else. He could shoot from the perimeter and blow past his man to the hoop.

The shooter—Marlon "Streakie" Johnson was the hired gun. At six-three tall, his outstanding long distance shooting demanded a zone defense to extend. On offense, I would isolate our big man to his side of the court or use him as a trailer on the fast break so he could easily position himself for a three-point shot.

The small forward—Chance "Gimme the Ball" Jordan, at six-three tall, was a great offensive rebounder and his biggest strength was slashing to the hoop. Usually, he was the finisher on the fast break. A lot of practice time was involved in getting the ball to the right player on the fast break, which would result in a lay-up. He was brilliant at the "one-on-one" drill. The one-on-one drill meant absorbing the foul and having the strength and determination to finish the shot.

The power forward—Malik "Nutty Head" Keys, at six-three tall, probably didn't weigh 180 pounds; but he played big. That is why I could afford to play him at the power forward position. I spent a lot of one-on-one time with him for his free throw shooting. He spent a lot of time running laps in practice because it took him a long time to make the required 70 percent or seven out of ten required at the end of practice. Five laps was the penalty for failure to accomplish that percentage.

The center—Derrick "Tough Guy" Martin, at six-four tall, brought toughness to the team. I used to tease him when I would say, "If you are scared, dial 911." In practice, he would be the one I picked to demonstrate the techniques of boxing out. I would box him out to show the importance of positioning when boxing out someone bigger and stronger. When we had to set-up, I wanted the ball to go through him. My philosophy was to work the ball in and then out as a basic rule. However, always take what the defense allows.

I was very disappointed with my team's play in the first half of the championship game. We were down by twelve at the half. I was so angry. I did not even bother to take them to a locker room. I used a hallway instead. I demanded everyone's undivided attention. As everyone stood around me, I signaled out the starting five and asked each, "How many free throws did you miss?" For my second question, I asked, "How many lay-ups have you missed?" Exclusively, they answered two or three to both questions. Disgusted with their answers, I exclaimed, "Doggunit, with the number of free-throws and lay-ups we have missed, we should be up by twenty; yet we are down by twelve. I tell you what if you keep missing lay-ups and free-throws; you will be sitting on the bench next to me. I refuse to lose a game because you can't make free throws or lay-ups. When we go back out there, I want you to expend energy. Do not be afraid to win. Now, everyone sound-off with Pirates on three; one, two, three, Pirates!" Of course, my discussion with them was a bit more explicit because I needed to get my point across while soliciting their utmost attention. It was the same strategy I would use on the referees when I purposely received a technical foul when the team was playing lousy.

I could not have scripted the second half any better than the team actually performed. Immediately, the trap defense provided the opportunity for two three-point field goals. That cut the lead to six. The score kept fluctuating from six to four until the final quarter. In the last two minutes of the final quarter, I could see the weariness in the other team's eyes, especially when we stole the ball and tied the score. The opposing coach had to burn a time out to avoid a five-second violation for not getting the ball in. I was glad he called the time out because I could save my three for the last minute. Eventually, our opponents got the ball in, but they missed the shot with less than a minute to go. I called time out. My instructions were, "Pass the ball around because I want the clock down 'til the last ten seconds. Do not pass the ball to anyone acting like they are scared to catch the ball. Everyone must come toward the ball when the ball is being passed to you. They are playing a 3-2 zone defense; therefore, the middle will be open. Tarik, at ten seconds, Jordan will come to the free-throw line; and you will pass the ball to him. Jordan, once you receive the ball, you will be wide open for practically a free throw shot; but do not take it. Give a head and shoulder fake and drive to the hoop. You either make the basket or make the referee call a foul one way or another. In other words, go strong."

The play worked to perfection. Jordan drove the ball and made the basket. With about four seconds left, the other team called time out; this allowed me to set the defense. "First," I stated, "do not foul. Second, go to the 3-1-1. That way we will have a man on the ball, and they will not be able to get it in so easy. Watch out for the runner and baseball pass down the court. So as soon as we break huddle, Tarik, you are on the ball. Jordan, you are all the way back. And everyone else must get their respective positions on the press. If the ball gets behind you, you must sprint to catch up. Now, let's hear Pirates on three; one, two, three, Pirates!" After a second or two, the other team got the ball in. The receiver rushed down the court and got off a three-point shot. The ball appeared to be in slow motion. Both bleachers full of fans, both benches, referees, as a matter of fact, everyone and everything in the gymnasium seemed still as the ball went into the air and started coming down. It took a lifetime for the ball to come down. When it did, it hit the front of the rim, then it hit the back of the rim, and finally, it rattled out. That's when our bleacher of fans exploded and our players on and off the court ran around yelling and hugging each other. As for me, my cheap little two-piece suit was drenched with sweat from all the emotion and intensity I had exuded throughout the game. Physically, I let out a sigh of relief for I had successfully led my team to a perfect season.

Although the perfect season at an alternative school, did not gain respect from the larger city schools; however, it brought a feeling of togetherness and esprit de corps to HHC. With the prowess of a perfect season, I tried to convince the director of the intramural athletic department for public schools in Baltimore City to give us a chance to see what we could do against the rest of the city schools. Besides, many of the referees complimented me on how well my team played. During the season, they commented that we probably would beat many of the larger schools because of our team play. The director informed me, "We do not have the funds to do that." My question was, "What funds? It does not cost very much for transportation. I will secure the transportation." He answered, "We have to pay referees and other expenses; besides, you have had your tournament. Let the other schools have theirs." My last attempt was saying, "We are always talking about how bad the kids are. Yet we never give them an opportunity to prove themselves. Their participation in the tournament may provide them exposure. This may be an avenue for them to have something to hold on to and turn into success. It could spill over to the rest of the second-chance students." I knew I was reaching and he was not hearing it.

After the season, I began to focus more on the AJROTC program and to sincerely impose its mission: "To motivate young people to be better American citizens," keeping in mind the job of an AI is tough enough, and it can be even more frustrating when dealing with inner-city kids. In a lot of situations, female cadets/students in Baltimore City come into the program with at least one child; and some are quick to show their womanhood. Many AIs lives and careers have been destroyed because they placed themselves in compromising positions and committed acts unbecoming of a mature adult. In one case, an AI, after being accused of having sexual affairs with female cadets, did something one would think came out of a fictional horror story.

As the story was told to me, he set his car on fire and burned himself to death. I must admit that such actions have not been confined to the inner cities.

The most prestigious school systems have had their share of inappropriate sexual behavior or carnal knowledge offenses. Particularly, one high school in Northern Virginia in the vicinity of Washington DC had, in the eyes of many instructors, one of the most prestigious programs in the United States. That was until the AI was accused by a cadet's parent of having sex with her daughter. Although nothing concrete was ever proved, the AI found himself dismissed by the school. He ended up selling used cars, and the school's program never recovered from his demise.

Anyway, I feel that sometime deans, directors, principals, educators, and people in like positions are there for the wrong reasons. It takes passion, along with mental and physical fortitude, to assist students to gain opportunities for positive exposure. Just because one holds a title does not mean that they are best suited for the position. For instance, when someone accomplishes the title of a doctor, it does not constitute that the person is a competent doctor. I have served with military officers fresh out of school, who were highly educated but lacked the common sense to lead efficiently and proficiently. My opinion is that sometimes we have to think outside the box. This may allow problem students/subordinates a chance to think and grow. Moreover, they may become assets and not become a liability as a citizen. Let us not forget about the Karen Hunts and the Jonathan Smiths of the world. They need help, too. My experience in dealing with inner-city youngsters has led me to believe that they are the product of their environment. They are not as bad as they want to portray themselves. Many lack parental/adult guidance in doing the right thing. When they find someone who they believe cares, they tend to cling on to that individual.

Overall, I feel the education system in Baltimore City as well as in many of the other inner cities has to develop a program of education tailored to the needs of the environment. Additionally, state, city/county officials, and parents as well have to work together in order to create schemes that will interest our under-privileged youths. All must see to it that our younger generation is involved in constructive programs so that they may become assets rather than liabilities to our nation.

2 DANS

I Want My Mommy

I will never forget the day I saw my little sister whimpering while walking around barefooted on our hardwood floors with only a drooping diaper on her fragile body. Every now and then, she cried out, "I want my mommy," who was nowhere to be found.

Along with her, the rest of the children and I were blindsided by our mom's rash disappearance. I should have fitted this piece to a puzzle together years ago when a friend of my dad came to our house lit up. He banged on the door, and he yelled, "Dan, come out of there, you son of a female dog (not so inexplicit). You know what you did to my sister." He called my father everything but a child of God. After he made such a fuss, someone let him in. The man tried to swing on my dad a few times, but he was inebriated to the point of falling down every time he swung. Despite minutes of the man quarreling and throwing punches, no real damage occurred. Finally, my grandmother got involved and convinced him to leave. That unpleasant scenario was merely a precursor in the numerous surprises and disappointments our family would inevitably face.

Water Valley

It was somewhat of a surprise when the day came for me to show proof of birth. Until then, I believed Memphis to be my birthplace. From viewing my birth certificate, the stork dropped me off in the small town of Water Valley, Mississippi. Additionally, my birth certificate brought to my attention that the suffix "Junior" was misspelled and placed in the middle of my full name as Junor. By the time I learned of the aforementioned information, I was a teenager, and I had an interest in visiting my birthplace.

Water Valley is located a little over an hour-and-a-half driving distance south of Memphis. As an adult, I ventured there on two previous occasions. On one occasion, I attended grandmother's funeral; and on the other occasion, I attempted to gain facts on her origin. More importantly, I wanted to trace our Indian ancestry.

My search ended after finding out many vital records were mysteriously burned with the town's library. Browsing through property records at the town's city hall was the last resort. The only name recognizable in those records was Uncle Henry's. Land was titled in his name. I knew him when I was a young boy in Memphis. I collected worms for him because I knew he liked fishing. To this day, I can see a vision of the big smile that lit up his big, round face. It was probably because of my thoughtful gesture and not the worms. He, too, had passed on before my last visit to Water Valley. As I drove about the town, I took routes that eventually led me to the address in proximity to where we once lived. I was a baby when we left Water Valley. The only place I vaguely remembered was grandma's grave site because I was an adult when we buried her. Like the rest of the land, weeds and wildflowers had overtaken the gravesite as well. I tried to visualize the place that used to be our home before we moved to Memphis.

THE HOMESTEAD

We must have moved close to Memphis between the latter part of 1952 and 1953. We lived in a farmed area not far from Millington. Often, images of a farm consisting of corn fields, cotton fields, chickens, pigs, horses, and cows creep into my mind. Deer, mice, snakes, possums, skunks, porcupines, wild cats, and other creatures took refuge in the nearby wooded areas as well. I never knew if the property was ours or if we were homesteaders working the land for the white man. Periodically, one would show up and act as though he was conducting a survey or an inspection. Once, I walked the land with him and my grandfather. Besides crops, the land contained a lot of edible and non-edible vegetation. Edible items like walnuts, pecans, plums, grapes, blackberries, etc. were just a few natural luxuries we looked forward to.

BOYS WILL BE BOYS

My cousins, Sonny, Harry, and I were always scouting for stuff to eat. Our ages ranged from three to five years. We were very mischievous. Curiosity almost killed the cats when one day Sonny and I dared each other to taste a piece of green wide-leafed vegetation. Why did we do that? It burnt our mouths so bad. We started running, crying, and screaming. Finally, someone slowed us down long enough to diagnose our problem. We ended up at the hospital. Later, we found out that the plant we ate was called elephant ears. It was poisonous. Everyone breathed a sigh of relief when we pulled through it.

There would be other naughty happenings involving us. See, where we lived, black children lacked constructive things to do back then. We lived in a small house within a rural area west of Memphis. The property featured a barn. Some of our mischievous doings took place there. Inside the barn, I was dared again. This time, they dared me to place my head under my cousin's dress and lick the split between her legs. Harry demonstrated the act for me. I never saw whether he actually performed the act. However, I placed my head under her dress, and I faked like I did it. I was not about to stick my tongue there. My female cousin snitched on me, and they teased me and called me a scaredy-cat. From that moment on, oral sex would never be part of my sexual activity.

MY SEXUAL ASSAULT

We began to split up when grandfather died. We moved to an even smaller house in Shelby County, more south of Memphis. Although the house was small inside, I appreciated the fruits of the land. The apple trees, fig trees, and even wild grape vines provided us with more of nature's small but delicious treasures. We resided there about two years before moving to a newer development not far from there. The development was known as Crocket Homes. Much like previous quarters, our house was often shared. The three-bedroom, one-bathroom shotgun house was very crowded. My mother, father, grandmother, and, many times, transient aunts and cousins lived there. With people piled atop each other, sleeping conditions were tight. One might find himself sleeping in the same bed with a sister or female cousin. I never thought much of that situation until the night I was sexually molested by an older female cousin. It is a hurting feeling when one keeps a degrading assault inside for years. I do not know why I did not tell anyone. However, I did feel a strange kind of fear and embarrassment. I cannot remember how I ended up in the same room with her because my younger brother and my five sisters lived in the house too. I am not sure if I was a teenager or not when the assault took place. Memories of my past are sometimes clouded in my mind.

THE BULLIES

Anyway, I was born on January 10, 1953, as Dan K. Berry. I assumed I was the third eldest of eight siblings. When the old cliché "the blacker the berry, the sweeter the juice" was written, I believe the Creator had me in mind. My somewhat shy disposition was overshadowed by my inner spirit of not being defeated in any kind of competition. Being dark skinned, I had many nicknames such as Shine and Two Shades. "Two shades blacker than me" was a phrase used most often by one of the neighborhood bullies, particularly the one we called Bear. He was big, black, and he limped because one leg was shorter than the other. Bear never failed to try to intimidate the smaller and younger guys in the neighborhood. Although he often called me names, I really never had a problem with him. Yet I always anticipated that we would someday come to fisticuffs. That encounter did not happen with him, but it did happen with someone just as big from our neighborhood.

The fight took place at school, right before my last period class. I was drinking water at the fountain in the school hallway when I was shoved. I turned around, and there was Big Sam with a gang of guys; so I asked, "What's up?" I continued to drink from the fountain. He shoved again. Now I am frustrated, and I made my mind up that if he shoves me again, I am going to turn around and hit him as hard as I can. My mindset was to get one good lick in. He shoved and I hit. Immediately, I had a problem. I kept forgetting he was left-handed. I would have fared much better if I had just realized that one small oversight. The fight lasted a few minutes before we were pulled away from each other. In a daze, I staggered to my French class. That class consisted of so many pretty girls, and it seemed every one of them was staring at me. Pretty girls were the only reason I enrolled in the class in the first place. Mad and antsy, I did not sit there very long before I jumped up. I ran for home because I knew my dad had a 22 caliber pistol hidden somewhere in his room. I was going for it. When I got home, it did not take long to find it. The problem took place as I was leaving back out. My grandmother cornered me. She started questioning me "What's wrong with you? What happened to your face?" I explained to her what happened. She said, "Next time do not stand there and let someone hit you in the face like that. You have to move. And what do you have there? Give me that gun, boy." Finally, after listening to her and calming down, I gave it to her. She always had a way of handling me, and I would never dispute my grandmother.

The next day, I wore shades to school so no one could see my black eyes. I was not in the mood for discussing what happened. I tried to stay clear of anyone who may unintentionally or intentionally provoke me into another fight. I was on a short fuse. As time went on, I realized the one thing I gained from that fight was respect. I may not have won the fight but, throughout the entire school, people knew I fought Big Sam and I defended myself well. I did not have the worry of being picked on anymore.

At the time, I was the oldest boy in the household. As I mentioned before, I was also the blackest person. All the other siblings' skin tones are much lighter than mine. If you look close enough, you can see the blue rings around the pupils of my eyes. In the sunlight, the blueness is more pronounced. I attribute that characteristic along with my high cheek bones to my grandmother and her native American-Indian ancestors. I have maintained a slim build throughout my life. I was a fast runner and considered myself very athletic. As a youngster, I was always an unofficial leader when it came to sandlot sports. I would go around the neighborhood rounding the fellows up to get a game on.

Depending on the season, we played baseball, football, or basketball. We were so poor that we used improvised equipment. We played with cork screws for balls, sticks for baseball, frisbees for footballs, balled-up rags for balls, and trash cans for baskets. Once, we set fire to an open field to create an area we could play all three sports. When the firemen showed up, they asked us if we knew how the fired started. We told them that we did not know but we were just trying to put it out. They commended us for our efforts and cautioned us about the dangers of the fire, particularly, the carbon dioxide fumes. The fumes were something we never thought about. Besides, the firemen probably knew it was us. We constructed our sports venue after the fire. We needed a place to go outside our homes. Our parents were glad to see us gone, especially in our household.

The Berry Family

At first glance, the make-up of our household and family appeared to be normal. Ultimately, the dynamics of our family's household would turn out to be far more than just typical. My immediate siblings consisted of six girls and two boys.

Although Susan is the oldest, her lack of mental maturation caused her to be overly meticulous. She is a worry wart, and at times, she would become highly emotional. Occasionally, we attended church. Prior to sitting down, I played musical chairs with my sisters and brother because no one wanted to sit next to Susan. She would always get the "spirit." Once the " spirit" hit her, she would fall to the floor and pass out.

In contrast to Susan, Mattie was as sly as a fox. On several occasions, I would catch her kissing the boys. While playing ball, Mattie was hit in the nose. Her nose never shrunk.

After Mattie, Lois was the next girl in line. Her petite size and flexibility earned her a place on the high school pep squad.

Like me, Jeremiah was fast. One day, he cut his foot on broken glass while running through a grassy field. He received several stitches. Similar to Susan and Mattie, Jeremiah had a space between his top two front teeth.

Shanice did not have a space between her two front teeth, but she had a supernumerary tooth. The supernumerary tooth would never affect her beauty. With her quiet disposition and long black hair, she was blessed with some of the American Indian features inherited from our grandmother.

Next, Cathie was even more petite than Lois. She was the youngest left in the household at the time our mother took flight, and she had become the Miss I-must-have-everything-perfect-before-I-go-to-school type girl. A funny thing happened one day. After all the prancing, fixing, and staring in the mirror, she stepped on an icy driveway and fell. The alligator tears rolled from her eyes. I felt sorry for her, but the entire event was very amusing. I can recall that wintry day, waiting to walk her to school. She almost made me late because every little strand of hair had to be fixed. Every little wrinkle had to be ironed out. Not to mention her little "leggies" (pantyhose) had to blend in with the rest of her clothes. As soon as she took about two steps onto the neighbor's driveway, *bam,* she slipped and fell. As much as I wanted to, I tried as hard as I could to refrain from laughing.

The youngest of the siblings was Lucie. She was about one year old when she was carried away from the little shot gun house by our mother. I never saw her again until she was grown—that was during a holiday season, around Christmas and New Year's Day, when our family got together.

The Intruders

Christmas time around Berry's residence was a very anxious time. My Uncle Bill would always remind me of how I fell from a high porch on Christmas day. At the time, I was an infant, and I broke my arm while reaching for an orange. The days at the little shotgun house brought even more disappointing holidays for us before the departure of our mom. The highlight of our anticipation was finding the toys we thought were hidden from us. We tried to figure out who was getting what. Dolls, bicycles, tricycles, electric train sets, and other items were just a few gifts we discovered. Bafflingly, on Christmas Day, all we received was a sock or stocking filled with a small amount of rock candies, nuts, apple, or orange. We were in a state of bewilderment. We asked each other, "What happened to the toys?"

Subsequently, we encountered many years of empty Christmases before the mystery began to unravel. The initial clue appeared when we saw our expectant mother leave with Lucie. She expedited herself to Slaton, Texas. At first, we did not see a valid explanation for her actions. However, the mystery unveiled in its entirety with the days to come. Our home at 4835 Motley Road became a *Nightmare on Elm Street*. Here she came, Susan Hart with plenty of baggage. The baggage featured the other Dan accompanied by Ben and Leonard. Now the picture was very clear. "Papa was a rolling stone." That's right. Our father was leading two different lives with two different families.

Susan quickly established herself as the queen bee of the household even though my grandmother was still there. However, the mole on her nose and her personality easily matched that of a wicked witch who so badly wanted us to disappear.

She and her boys moved in as though we had intruded upon their world. Their anger was very obvious. Leonard was a spoiled brat. He was the youngest, and he wanted to be left alone. Selfishness has always been his strongest trait. Short in stature, he, too, was a good athlete, and he hated to lose. Older than Leonard was Ben. He tolerated us more. In fact, Ben and I acquired a decent relationship considering the circumstances. Ben had been around the block a few times, and he knew more about street life than me. In other words, I was more naïve than him when it came to girls, gangs, cars, motorcycles, and things. He drove the truck when we hauled cardboard boxes for my dad's self-created cardboard business. We salvaged the cardboard from companies discarding it and sold it to companies demanding it. Ben and I came up with a plan of upgrading the business to make a more lucrative amount of cash. Before we implemented our strategy, I decided to join the army.

The segregation of both families was very volatile and created an even more crowded living condition. We slept all atop each other, and we barely got enough to eat. Many nights, we went to bed hungry. The intruders treated us like trash. However, Susan never failed to ensure that her kids got the best of what little we had.

The real insult for me was not only that there is another family set but I had a brother by the same first name. He was only a couple of months older than me. Like Leonard, he was short, and the only difference was his bow legs. He had outstanding baseball skills. His skills earned him a baseball scholarship from a college in Alabama. Eventually, he got a girl pregnant and dropped out of college. To add injury to insult, the girl came to live in the shot gun house with us too.

Regardless of Big Sue's dislike for Barbara, she and Little Dan got married anyway. However, the marriage did not last very long with the interference of Big Sue. Being divorced, Little Dan began to enter into one relationship after another. Although he was the baby daddy to children by multiple women, he never actually fathered anyone. Today, he still resides with Big Sue and several of his children in the house I once called home. At this point in his life, he speaks as though he is seeking a deity, yet I fail to see him practice what he preached. His situation is a reflection of "the more things change, the more they remain the same."

FLEEING THE COOP

In yesteryears, Big Sue never required Dan to find his own place nor get a job. Discriminately, she practically forced little Susan and Mattie out of the house. Consequently, both said "I do" and married at an early age to the first person with the tiniest glimmer of kindness. I do not think that love had anything to do with it. Eventually, both marriages ended in divorce.

Little Susan's ex-husband, Anis Strange, was as spooky and idiosyncratic as his name suggested. Before their divorce, he and Susan moved into a house not far from where we grew up. On one of my visits home from the Army, I went to see them. It was like a scene from an Alfred Hitchcock movie. Anis was locked up in a dark room. He was hiding under the covers as if someone was after him. When he realized it was me, we talked; and as we talked, he kept looking around. I summed his disposition up as one of the two following rationales: he displayed symptoms of drug-related paranoia or he was some kind of undercover agent.

On the other hand, Mattie married Don. Don was a slickster. One had to decipher his truths from the lies he told. When he spoke to you, he smiled, showcasing a gold crown centered with the outline of a star on his right central incisor. His interests were always Cadillac cars, gambling, and crooked deals. He and Mattie managed to have three children at an early age. Big Susan's plan to force all the Berrys to leave their nest prematurely one after another worked well.

In retrospect, the shame of having a half-brother with the same name and an overcrowded house overwhelmed me. In the summer of 1971, I graduated from high school. Immediately, I joined the Army.

LITTLE JAMES

It was during a temporary duty assignment at Fort Sam Houston, Texas, that I decided to locate my grandmother (on my mother's side of the family). By that time, my mother had retreated back to Memphis. I boarded a bus headed for Slaton, Texas. The wintry mixed made the route very scenic. The ride was so tranquil with the snow-covered countryside. The icicles hung from the trees. Wild animals, particularly deer, crossed the bus's path every now and then.

Several hours elapsed when the bus entered the town's limits. Slaton was a small "one horse" town. The streets were covered with snow. It was like déjà vu. I had never seen my grandmother before. Instantly, I could tell by the look in her eyes. She was standing at the bus stop. After confirming our relationship, I hugged and kissed her the first time in my life. My grandmother was a thin, slim woman. She was light skinned, energetic, and looked extremely healthy for her age. She appeared very much in control of all of her mental and physical faculties. Surprisingly, she could even drive.

She provided me with the 411 as she drove to the house. It was a very quick tour of the whole rural town. Amid the tour, she pointed to an old shack. She said, "Ya' ma lived there alone with little brother, James, before he passed away. Ya' sister, Lucy, stayed with me and grandpa."

Heretofore, I heard bits and pieces of the story concerning James's death. Now, I was getting it firsthand from my grandmother. A solemn, hapless feeling came over me as I sat quietly listening and analyzing her every word. Finally, we arrived at her home. It was a tiny, cottage-style house. She and her roommate made me feel welcomed. I spent the time capturing all the details of the occurrences leading up to James's death. Before I realized it, the weekend was over, and I had to return back to post. The memories of my grandmother and the story she told made such an impression on me that I put it in the words in the following lyrics:

Little James

As I looked outside the
    window,
many thoughts ran
through
    my mind.
I was headed for Texas.
Didn't know what I would
find.
The "Greyhound" bus
    pulled up to the
station.

The streets were all
covered
    with snow.
It was a small town
called
    "Slaton."
It seemed I had been
there
    befo'.

My Grandma stood there
    awaitin'.
I could tell by the
look in
    her eyes.
You could see our
relations,
As she began to cry.

It was late, late in the
    evenin',
when grandma, she cried.
I didn't wanna believe it.
Little James, he died.
It was late, late in the
    evenin',
when grandma, she cried.
I didn't wanna believe it.
Little James, he died.
Little James, he died.

As we drove to her home,
She pointed to an old
    shack.
Ya' ma' lived there
    alone.
She left and she never
    came back.
Your sister, Lucie, she
    stayed,
with me and grandpa.
She never could behave,
but it wasn't really her
    fault.

It was late, late in the
     evenin',
when grandma, she cried.
I didn't wanna believe it.
Little James, he died.
It was late, late in the
     evenin',
when grandma, she cried.
I didn't wanna believe it.
Little James, he died.
Little James, he died.

After the weekend,
I boarded the bus for
     home,
watching grandma from
the
     window,
as she stood there
     alone.
I will never forget the
look
     she had,
nor the feeling I had
     inside.
The reality was too much
     to bear,
so I began to cry.

It was late, late in the
     evenin',
when grandma, she cried.
I didn't wanna believe it.
Little James, he died.
It was late, late in the
     evenin',
when grandma she cried.
Little James just wasn't
     eatin'.
Little James, he died.
Little James, he died.

BEN'S DEATH

I was on emergency leave when I took my next trip. Memphis was my destination. This time, I was stationed in Korea. An unexpected death forced me to fly home immediately. I remember sitting in the co-pilot seat of a chopper flying through the mountains of the demilitarized zone (DMZ). It was like I was in a daze from wondering why I am being flown back to Memphis. Our unit had been on the DMZ for almost two weeks, and it was winter time. Not to mention, we conducted all our missions at night with frequent snowfalls. Inexplicably, I could hear the North Korean soldiers on their loudspeakers cry out, "Sergeant Berry from Memphis, Tennessee, go home." Trenches were dug out around the mountains; sometimes, we slept inside the trenches in our sleeping bags. Some mornings, we would wake up buried in snow. This time, my stay on the DMZ was interrupted.

The Red Cross notified my unit of my brother's death. Ben was riding a motorcycle at the time of the accident. As I recall, a woman turned her automobile from a side street onto the highway in front of him. The incredible thing about the whole incident was when I realized the identity of the woman.

Isn't it ironic that the woman was the mother of a girl I wrote lyrics about on a previous occasion? The girl and I were schoolmates. She was so highly astute that I thought that she had it all together. Her real self unfolded when I just happened to be downtown in Memphis one afternoon. It was on Beale Street near W. C. Handy Park. One of my friends pointed her out. I did not realize who she was before that moment. She wore a brunette-colored wig with tons of makeup and eye shadow. The mini-skirt she wore was skin tight and barely covered what little butt she had. Her little scrawny legs were draped with black fishnet panty hose and long black leather high-heeled boots. That day was the last time I saw her. For obvious reasons, neither daughter nor mother showed up at any of the funeral services.

The following lyrics portray my thoughts of her:

Pleasure Provider

I remember when we were
in
    high school.
She always seemed to
keep
    her cool.
She did homework so very
    smartly.
She would receive an A
    or B.

She was so quiet, she
was so
        fine.
She had problems that
        wrecked her mind.

I felt she solved them
time after time.
I had no clue she was
stuck
        in a bind.

The fancy clothes,
make-ups
        and lipsticks,
don't cha know, cannot
hide
        her.
It's plain to see,
everyone
        knew her score but me.
She is a price tag
pleasure
        provider, a
pleasure
        provider.

When she came on the
        scene,
it struck my last nerve.
A stretch limo' pulled
up to
        the curb.
She sported diamonds
while
        draped in furs.

She was so quiet, she
was so
        fine.
She had problems that
wrecked her mind.
I felt she solved them
time after time.

I had no clue she was
stuck
        in a bind.

The fancy clothes, make-
ups, and lipsticks,
don't cha know, cannot
hide
        her.

It's plain to see,
everyone
        knew the score but me.
She is a price tag
pleasure
        provider, a
pleasure
        provider.

(Rap)

She is a pleasure
provider,
A price tag pleasure
        provider,
pacing streets day and
        night,
with her long red boots
and a mini-skirt so
tight.
She ducks and dodges
        5-0 by the minute.
Sneaking in motels and
lodges

to let some chump get up
        in it.
No time to converse
'cause it
        is not her style.
Acting like he is her
first,
        just tripping like a child.
She jumps out of cabs

>   without paying her
> fare.
>
> Taxi drivers cannot find
> her
>   anywhere.
> She wears many
> disguises,
>   while committing
> her
>   crime.
> Sleeping in high rises
>   without paying a
> dime,
> When it comes to trust
> no one can confide in
> her.
>
> Everyone knew her score
> but
>   me.
> She is a price tag
> pleasure provider,
> a pleasure provider,
> a price tag pleasure
> provider,
> a pleasure provider.

> **"And, ye fathers, provoke not your
> children to wrath: but bring them
> up in the nurture and admonition"**
> **of the Lord**. Ephesians 6:4

Although the funeral brought our family a little closer together, I never forgave my father for creating a dual family atmosphere. Nonetheless, he allowed my brother and me to have the same name. Even today, I have been considering changing my name. Literally, I have been insulted because of my name and because of my height. Not to mention my dark skin in contrast to everyone else in the family. Little Dan's daughters made the statement, "Big Dan, I do not know who you look like." Abruptly, I responded, "I look like myself." For the record, as embarrassing as the situation has been for me, my heart will always cherish the fact that we have the same blood. No one can change that. Moreover, we as a family must move on. It is highly important that we care for each other and respect each other. Much like all families, we did not have a choice in the manner of which we were brought into this world. The truth of the matter was that our parents created this situation well before we moved to Memphis. Additionally, if I was born in Mississippi, my father had to do a lot of traveling back and forth.

In the after light of Dan Senior's shocking surprises, many residual mental effects linger in our family. Those residual effects are confirmed when I confer with my sisters. However, speaking on my own behalf, I took the things he let happen to us and used them to create vows of what I will or will not do. I vowed not to let my children's Christmas be empty and lack the joy of the season. I ensure that I buy gifts for my children on their birthdays although they are grown at this point of our lives. I do not call them only when I need money or something from them. I try to communicate with them and show concern for what is happening in their lives and their children's lives, whether it is positive or negative. On the other hand, Dan Senior would call me during times like Christmas when money was tight and ask for hundreds up to thousands of dollars. I would always send it to him, but all I wanted was for him to call sometime to see how I and my family were doing. The aforementioned are only a few lessons from a laundry list I learned from Dan Senior. I learned more lessons from Little Dan.

Little Dan talked one way but walked another. He talked about righteousness, but his actions were au contraire. Whenever I saw him, usually, he had the deer-in-the-headlight look. Because he had multiple "baby mommas," many of his kids were left to fend for themselves. He lacked responsibility for his actions because he always had a crush. When the going got rough, he could fall back on his mother. He was constantly in and out of the house burdening Big Susan with the responsibility of raising his kids. For the most part, I have always been sympathetic with Big Susan; however, she disappointed me when she allowed Little Dan to con Little Susan to cosign for him to buy a car. Little Dan fell behind on the monthly payments, so the lending institution corralled Little Susan, who ended up paying for the car. From Little Dan's laissez-faire attitude and negative behavior, he helped me to solidify my intentions of taking care of my own affairs and my own children.

As one can see from the tumultuous lives of the two Dans, I was able to draw from them things I did not wish to do in order to raise my children in a manner whereby I am satisfied with the elements and environment I have provided, just so they may live prosperous lives.

OUR MA DEAR

Years later, the death of my father would bring us all together again. On the day of the funeral, an utmost embarrassing moment occurred when my biological mother showed up. At the church, she was determined to capture the limelight as part of the immediate family. During the procession of daughters and sons, she jumped ahead of everyone. My step-sister tried to convince her that she was not supposed to be in line with us. She was not hearing that. For some reason, she had the attitude as if she had the right to be there. Her drama did not end there. She pulled another antic when she went up to view my dad lying in his casket. Why did she bend to kiss him on the cheek? Evidently, the kiss was not enough. After the funeral, she included herself in one of the limousines with my stepmother and her children for the ride to the cemetery.

I guess the antics that Ma Dear (as we always called my mother) pulled appeased her for bearing nine children for the man. Although she bore his children, she left us at a time children needed their mother, especially my sisters. I am the only one who kept a decent relationship with her; however, I was overseas a lot. For the most part, she always lived alone, and she did not bother to communicate with the girls. Presently, she continues her same ways, much like dad used to do but with a more sly mannerism; she calls us when she needs something. Even with post cards priced at a dollar these days, she does not think to send her children or grandchildren a fruit for thought. Acknowledging birthdays with a phone call would not break her.

Needless to say, it has always been about her. So it was no surprise when one of my sisters told me that after more than four decades and after she has been married at least three more times, she was trying to get some of dad's social security money. Now, ain't she a piece of work?

Although she displayed an unexpected irrational behavior, it soon became overshadowed when a strange young lady showed up at the funeral wanting to see her dad for the last time. So even from his grave, Dan Senior left his ambiguous families with another one of his big surprises.

3 HOTS AND A COT

The Community

"I was at a urinal when I was approached by two or more people. They came up behind me and grabbed me. I struggled but I could not overcome their force. Lowering me to my knees, someone held me down while the other person forced his penis into my mouth. He demanded me to suck on it. After a while, he started ejaculating. I felt something salty and slimy going down my throat. I almost choked on it." The aforementioned statement was part of an inmate's record of trial. I gained access to his file as the noncommissioned officer in-charge (NCOIC) of the dental treatment facility within the institution. I conducted interviews for the purpose of training inmates to work at the DTF among other functions.

It is an understatement to say that the NCOIC of a DTF encompasses a vast array of duties and responsibilities. Safeguarding and maintaining dental records are critical aspects of the job. Much like medical records, dental records must be handled with the strictest confidence. Moreover, the contents of dentals are sometimes used to identify bodies. In many cases, a person's body is so mutilated or burned that dental radiographs (x-rays) are the last resort for identification. This type of identification has been most common in combat situations, making it mandatory for all military personnel to have a panoramic dental x-ray. Nonetheless, identification by dental x-rays is used in garrison and civilian cases as well.

Later, I would find out first handed about positive identification utilizing x-rays. As NCOIC at a clinic in Texas, I had to release dental records to a criminal investigator. He was investigating the death of a military spouse. Her husband was a medic suspected of cutting her up. Body parts were in dumpsters from Waco to San Antonio. Therefore, it was a need-to-know for the investigation to secure her dental records to view her x-rays.

Prior to that incident, I was the custodian of the dental records of personnel treated within the institution; therefore, it was vital to keep accurate and updated records. One never knows what can happen in a prison environment. Besides, at this military confinement facility, every day had the potential for disaster within the prison environment and the surrounding towns as well.

Anyway, the facility is located in Leavenworth County (just north of the city of Leavenworth, Kansas) in the upper northeast portion of the state. It has been in operation for over 170 years. The fort occupies 5,600 acres (23 km²) and 7,000,000 ft² (650,000 m²) of space in one thousand buildings and one thousand five hundred quarters.

Right outside Fort Leavenworth's gates stands the infamous Leavenworth Federal Penitentiary. Its huge, white, brick building and high barbed wire fences made it impossible to miss. The grounds are accentuated by the presence of several huge black buffalo grazing on the grass. It is amazing how the buffaloes make the prison seem a bit of laissez-faire.

The federal penitentiary houses civilian and former military inmates while the DB, now a maximum-security prison, houses convicted military personnel.

Their crimes are as simple as disrespect, to as serious as rape and murder. My assignment as the NCOIC of the dental treatment facility (DTF) was unique.

Although thousands of inmates are habitants of the DB, the communities outside its walls present more hostilities. The town of Leavenworth and its surroundings are saturated with a prison-related populace. Spouse, siblings, and significant others reside in those communities. They are there to support or await the release of an inmate. With that mix of people, one can sometimes unknowingly be faced with a life and death moment.

Wrong Places/Wrong Times

In saying that, it did not take me two weeks to find myself with my back against the wall due to a couple of events. Both could have ended fatal. Each time, I was indirectly set up by a fellow soldier, and I had no business being in either place.

The first event occurred after a card party. Like an immature teenager, I was influenced to participate by a chatty NCO. He was one of the first people I met on my arrival at my new duty station. Although I was assigned to a dental unit, we shared the barracks with a medical unit. SGT Smith was the supply NCO for both units. One of his duties was assigning rooms. My first impression was not to trust him. I soon found out that he enjoyed drinking and gambling with fellow soldiers. To my distress, I participated in both at the party.

When the party ended, I was under the influence of gin and juice. It was to the point of being reluctant to drive back to the barracks. A lady friend of the supply sergeant offered me a place to sleep it off. The drama unfolded once I was settled on the floor in her living room. A knock on the door and a voice calling, "Margaret, open the door." She answered the door and spoke very softly. I assumed she tried to get rid of him. He was not hearing that, so he shouted, "Who do you have in there?" She responded, "A friend, sleeping it off." With the tone of the man's voice, I decided it was time to leave. The last thing I wanted to do was get involved with a couple's relationship. What I thought would be a safe haven was quickly turning into a nightmare. I asked, "Is that your man or something?" She exclaimed, "No, I do not know why he is here this time of the morning." I apologized, "I am very sorry if I caused you any trouble. I think the best thing for me to do is leave." She tried to assure me with, "You do not have to. He will go away. I do not know why he is acting like this." I thanked her for her hospitality and got myself together. As I walked out of the door, the person questioned me, "What are you doing here?" I continued to walk to my car saying, "I was only trying to sober up before heading to post. That is it." Abruptly, he pulled out a gun and stated, "You best be moving on." Now I am staring down the barrel of a pistol. Because it was dark, I could not tell what kind of pistol he pulled. All I wanted to do was get out of his sight as fast as I could. Without a word, I eased inside the car and pulled off. I did not feel safe until I turned a corner and he was nowhere in sight.

After that encounter, I vowed not to get caught up like that again. I never imagined something like that would happen again. However, a couple of weeks passed and it did. It was at a house party in downtown Leavenworth. We were invited by a fellow soldier. Three of us rode together. When we walked into the apartment on the third floor, I saw a Mexican and two rednecks playing "eat the peg" on a hard wood floor in the kitchen. I insinuated that it may not be such a good idea to stay. Melvin, the driver, tried to reassure me with, "Timmy (a white soldier) invited us, so he knows these people." Still, I did not trust the environment. Melvin and I walked into the living room where the music was playing. A few people were dancing. The apartment was a cracker box so there was not very much room to move around. I took a position with my back to a wall where I could see the entrance to the living room. Thank God, I did. In no time at all, Spencer (the third soldier who came with us) yelled, "What are you guys doing?" Frantically, he rushed to the living room. The Mexican and the rednecks chased him. Suddenly, we were surrounded by them. We jostled with them until the Mexican pulled a knife and the rednecks drew pistols. Immediately, I tried to open a window. It was jammed so I broke the glass. I yelled to Melvin and Spencer, "Let's get out of here." I jumped through the window and they followed me. Fortunately for us, there was a store underneath the apartment with a canopy. I hit the canopy, rolled off of it to the ground, and they followed. The rednecks shot at us. It must have drawn the attention of the local police. We were stopped by them and questioned. We told them exactly what happened. They escorted us back to the car. By that time, the troublemakers had cleared out. The police cautioned us and informed us to get back to the fort.

That incident brought about retaliation by some of the soldiers from both medical and dental personnel on base. The white soldier who invited us to the party was cornered and forced to identify the people who assaulted us. After a few weeks, they were found and jacked up inside a grocery store. Strange mishaps and findings did not just occur in the communities. Many times, my days at the DB were somewhat unbelievably enlightening.

Along with many other duties, I had to screen inmates to work in the DTF. The process involved reviewing the would-be employee's record of trial. Needless to say, the information in the record of trial strongly supports the old cliché "sometimes the truth is stranger than fiction."

IF YA' STILL HERE
(From Death Row)

During my tour there, in the early '80s, I treated inmates on death row. Based on my ten years of being a soldier and having gone through many situations whereby I was discriminated against, I can honestly say that blacks were more likely to be imprisoned for things that their white counterparts would get a slap on the hand for. Imprisonment was just one of the punishments inflicted on the black soldiers. Other penalties such as non-judicial punishment—Article 15s, dishonorable discharges, extra duties, restrictions, reprimands, verbal and nonverbal counseling—were quickly applied as resolutions for many offenses that may not have even been misdemeanors in the civil world.

Anyway, our procedures for treating inmates on death row were completely different from those of the other inmates. For instance, the entire prison grounds had to be cleared before they were transported to the clinic. Therefore, we did not treat them in the midst of regular duty hours. We would return later that evening.

Inmates on death row arrived in hand cuffs and shackles. They were guarded by heavily armed soldiers. I recall my initial acquaintance with death row inmate, Eddie Matters. He was a dark-skinned black man. He stood approximately five feet seven inches tall, and he was turning bald. He could have used a shave because his beard was rugged. It was also short with black and gray hairs. His maxillary anterior (top front) teeth were missing.

He was convicted for the rape and murder of a fellow soldier's wife. The other inmates spread rumors of the incident. The whispers through the grapevine had Matters attempting to rape the woman. She gave in. After she saw what he pulled out, she began to laugh. That's when he killed her. The military police found him at Burger King. With her blood still on his hands, he was eating a hamburger.

Seeing him in my chair for treatment after hearing that story, I could not relieve my mind of it. My initial treatment (TX) was to place an amalgam restoration (silver filling) after the dentist drilled out the decay. Furthermore, I started his TX of scaling and root planning. As I conducted the TX, I informed him of the heavy calculus (calcified plaque) build-up on his teeth. He would have to come back for me to finish. My words were, "I am not able to complete your TX at this time. You have deep periodontal pockets with calculus; therefore, I need to bring you back for a more definitive scaling. If you are still here, I will complete your TX on the next visit." Matters smiled and looked at me as if to ask, "What do you mean if I am still here?"

A month later, he returned to the clinic. I was mildly surprised when he spoke. He opened up the conversation with, "I understand what you meant when you cleaned my teeth on the first visit. I could tell how smooth they were and how my gums began to heal. My mouth really felt good. I have been brushing and flossing more. I want to thank you for taking the time to perform such outstanding TX. I did not take it personal when you said if you are still here. I knew what you were trying to say. Again, thank you." After I performed the last bit of definitive scaling on inmate Matters, I never saw him again.

The case of inmate Matters was atypical to many of the black inmates. Inmates involved in lesser crimes swore that they were innocent and railroaded to prison. I have strong feelings that some were actually innocent. Moreover, I have witnessed that the punishments for black soldiers were more severe than that of white soldiers based on the sum of the same circumstances and crimes.

Yes, the military was like a mirror reflecting the same inequities, prejudices, and discriminations as minorities faced in mainstream America the "land of the free."

THE EMBEZZLER

Timothy McSweeney was the only Caucasian inmate that we hired. As a soldier, he worked in a United States Army Finance Office. He was arrested and convicted for embezzlement. He would never say much, and he always walked with a swagger. Periodically, I would pick his brains. Specifically, I wanted to know how he was able to embezzle thousands of dollars for such a long period of time before he was caught. One day, in a roundabout way and with a puzzled look, I asked him, "How in the world were you able to get away with thousands of dollars?" Carefully, he began by saying, "It was easy. I used the social security number of soldiers already separated from the military. Then I cut checks for them. Obviously, they never saw the checks because I managed to cash the checks. I never deposited money in a bank. I secured the money in a safe and reliable place." My next question was, "Is the amount of money worth the time spent in behind these walls." With a high degree of certainty, Timothy remarked, "Of course, based on good behavior, I will have to spend about eighteen months here. The amount of money by far outweighs any amount I would have been able to save by working for eighteen months." One could not feel sorry for Tim. Obviously, he had succeeded with a well-planned scheme, and he had no regrets.

THE INFORMER

Another inmate that worked for us was James Davis from Chicago, Illinois. He was tall, black, and had a short afro. He was the only inmate that I felt prepared himself once released. Often times, I witnessed him reading or studying for a test. He was easy to communicate with. Yet he was convicted of assault on a commissioned officer. I empathized with him because I could remember the many times I wanted to use my M16 to butt-stroke the head of one of those nonsense "butterballs." Just think if I followed through with my intentions, I would be in the same fix. Although it was not such a smart move, at least James had the courage to throw a punch. For some unknown reason, I never saw him become extremely mad.

On the contrary, James had the uncanny knack of acquiring information. I could depend on him to provide me with all the happenings that went on inside the walls. He knew the dirt on the guards as well as all the other inmates. Although I very seldom ate inside the walls, he informed me about an incident that made me not want to eat at their dining facility again. As he described it, one of the inmates tried to get back at the guards by putting human feces in the chili. Somehow, more people than the intended victims, including inmates, ate from that pot. The incident brought about an epidemic of hepatitis.

Other tidbits of information involved who's screwing who from inmates to guards. He pointed out inmates I never suspected of being homosexual. I never realized that we had one working in our midst. Before his workmate entered the clinic that morning, he warned me that I may not recognize him. Needless to say, James was right. From first glance, his face was so distorted from blows from someone's knuckles; I really did not recognize who he was. James blamed the beating on the inmate's boyfriend.

More surprisingly, he made me aware of female guards and female medical personnel screwing male inmates. He indicated himself as being involved with one of the females. The strangest thing was how inmates (male and female) relayed information to carry out their plan of having sex. They passed notes while in the library. Although male and female inmates were separated by a wall, they used the wall by carving a hole big enough to pass their notes. Moreover, the hole was big enough for a penis. How they succeeded in making out bewildered me, but James swore that it was true, and they did it on a regular basis. The grapevine spread stories very quickly within the walls. Moreover, inmates found out about happenings that I was not privy to. The fact that many worked outside the walls to earn small stipends helped them establish familiarity with outsiders. They worked jobs at places like the car wash, commissary, and lawns of post housing. In addition to the jobs, they participated in sports events such as football, softball, and basketball.

Some of the hardest-fought battles of tackle football were played between the inmates and the guards. The inmates never missed the opportunity to knock some of the guards on their backs. That was their subtle payback for the hard times some guards gave them. On those nights, the medics were as busy as bees. Although I did not have the opportunity to play football against the inmates, I opposed them in basketball. Many knew me from the dental clinic. Those who did not know me personally knew my reputation.

Not only was I the player-coach for our basketball team, but I was also the post's leading scorer. I averaged about twenty-eight points a game. I scored fifty-two in one game at a time where there were no three-point baskets. One of my fellow Masonic brothers watched me one night, and he informed me after an intense game that I hit thirteen shots in a row. I never knew that because I was so caught in just trying to win the game. I remember the game when we beat the inmates because I was fouled with zero seconds left on the clock. I had to make both free throws for the tie and send the game to overtime. In overtime, with approximately three minutes left and a three-point lead, I fouled out after scoring thirty-five points for the game. Although I was tired and drained, I had to focus strictly on my coaching duties. I realized three minutes was a lot of time for the inmates to overcome a three-point lead. I went to more of a deliberate approach by slowing the game down when we were on offense. Along with my team making their free throws and the stalled offense, we won the game.

After that game, I seemed to have gained a great deal of credibility with the inmates. Therefore, I never missed a chance to encourage them to take advantage of their opportunities during their sentencing. Many were interested in attending colleges. They had aspirations of receiving scholarships. Some college recruiters came to see a few of them play basketball. I encouraged the ones with a desire and the prerequisites to join the retraining brigade to do so. Indeed, there were success stories. However, as with many prisons, there were unpleasant ones as well. Monroe Sullivan's story was very degrading to himself and his victim.

PUNK?

Monroe Sullivan's record provided a highly explicit account of an act that caused his conviction. Monroe was an eighteen-year-old black man. He grew up in Los Angeles, California. Typically, he was a blueprint for more than 75 percent of the prison population. As a matter of fact, every Thursday, a line of inmates exceeding more than a quarter mile consisted of at least 75 percent of black men. They arrived from the prison located in Manheim, Germany. We commonly referred to the line as the Manheim connection.

Monroe had stood in that very line upon his arrival. He was convicted of sodomy. For one convicted of physically violating another person's body, his attitude was very cavalier. He acted as if he did not have a care in the world. Nonetheless, he was one of my selections to work at the dental clinic. It is an understatement to say that the officer-in-charge and I were in awe when we read inmate Monroe's record of the trial.

Knowing what I did about Monroe, one day, my curiosity got the best of me, so I asked Monroe, "Why did you make another man suck your penis?" He replied, "Because he was a punk." Then I asked him, "What does that make you?" I repeated, "You forced another man to suck your penis. What does that make you, a punk or faggot?" Again, he answered, "He was a little white punk, and I proved it." I retorted, "The only thing you proved was that you have a twisted mind! Was it worth it? You are incarcerated for at least another three years. Tell me, was it worth it?" Surprisingly, he said, "Yes."

He went on to say, "I get three hot meals, a bunk, and I get twenty-five dollars' worth of goods such as cigarettes, toilet articles, and other necessities. Besides, the work at the DTF is not hard." I then quipped, "What about your freedom? Do you value your freedom?" He remarked, "I do not have anything to go back to LA for. I am comfortable here." Before that moment, it was hard for me to believe that anyone would be satisfied with being incarcerated. However, I did not give up on Monroe. Every chance I got, I tried to convince him to look at the positive aspects of being free.

Truly, I felt that he was not a bad person, only immature. He was the type to follow scandalous people.

CALVIN KERR, JR.

Out of all the happenings at the DB—scandals involving sex and sodomy, money, drugs, brutal beatings, food sabotage (feces in chili)—the one thing that really puzzled me was the "three hots and a cot" theory of Monroe. I am mystified by the number of trifling; inmates were content with having three free meals and a bunk. I feel safe to say that as long as there are prisons and inmates, stuff will happen. Sure, other privileges such as the twenty-dollar commissary one at the DB is included. Is not the price of freedom worth more than those minuscule privileges and three hots and a cot?

WHO'S LOVING KATIE

The Drill Team

Weeks passed and Katie was not in school. I called and called. After numerous futile attempts, she answered her cell phone. Finally, I got a chance to talk to her. Before she could utter a complete sentence, she began to cry. Moreover, what she had to say immediately brought tears from my eyes. As I deciphered her words, I began putting two and two together.

I figured the tragedy had to occur on a very cumbersome and extended day for me. Other members of our esteemed drill team and I practiced for hours synchronizing our competitive routines. The first sergeant (Top) pulled me to the side. He acted very strange and very serious, which was a bit out of character. Here is a man that never misses an opportunity to deliver a wise crack or an insult. My curiosity really set in when he did not joke about the size of my big mouth or head. I knew something bad must be going on. Especially when he was monotonic as he requested, "Cadet Sergeant Manuel, if you have the time, I would like for you to stay with Cadet Private Katie Wright until someone arrives to pick her up." I assured him, "Of course I will." My answer was a no-brainer because Katie was my best friend. I wanted to stay with her; besides, I recruited her. It took me awhile convincing her to join our Army Junior Reserve Officer Training Corps (AJROTC).

She started in the ninth grade. The year after our program distinguished itself as an honor unit. Honor unit is the second highest rating a school could achieve based on its annual inspection. On an annual inspection, all aspects of the program are inspected to including logistics, administration, operations, public affairs, personnel, and training. I was the cadet personnel noncommissioned officer in-charge (NCOIC) of Charlie Company. I kept records of every cadet assigned to Charlie. The records included but not limited to documentation of the following items: promotions, demotions, awards, letters of recommendations/ commendations, and proof of participation. It was highly pertinent to keep an accurate account of events that members of our battalion attended. Attendance and participation was a critical area in passing or exceeding the mark for the inspection. Extra-curricular events such as drill competitions, Raider team challenges, color guard, spelling bees, and other academic items affected our status. Therefore, our drill team was an integral part of securing honor unit status, and I was a member of it as well. As a high school student, it gave me a sense of pride to be an asset to our unit.

Now my best friend is practicing beside me, and I want her to become a viable asset. I want her to overcome whatever she is going through. Furthermore, it provides the perfect opportunity for us to spend more time together. The esprit de corps of the team just might give her a sense of belonging. No doubt, she will be part of a highly polished machine whose reputation spreads from Baltimore to Richmond.

At a highly renown high school in Northern, Virginia, a place profiling the movie *Remember the Titans*, our team revealed its outstanding prowess by winning a school record of fourteen trophies. We took home only eleven of them because the host school ran out of first place trophies. Therefore, to this date, we never received three of the fourteen trophies we won.

Anyway, I knew that we will continue to participate in drill events and win again. I wanted Katie to someday stand with me as we receive our trophies. This will provide us with a common thread as friends. We had nothing in common until I decided to invade her island and become her confidant. My goal was for her to one day look me in the eyes and talk to me. Believe me, I am not the type to compliment other females. However, she is very attractive. With catlike, light blue eyes and naturally long blonde hair, her physique exemplifies a typical model. Her shortcomings were not in her looks.

I thought her deficiencies were in direct correlation with her mental faculties. Just differentiating between her left and right to execute drill movements was a real challenge for her. It took more time for her to learn, so she had to work harder than everyone else. Top, our army instructor (AI), would often say, "Katie, I mean your military right. I'm gonna put a rock in your right hand to help you remember." No matter how hard she tried, Katie could not consistently execute the movements. In time, I became her one on one trainer. Top yelled, "Cadet Sergeant Cynthia Manuel, go and work with Katie Wright!" I guess he felt that since Katie and I were friends, I could help her better.

Besides, he never missed a chance to keep me occupied. He always said that I talked too much, and he never failed to tease me about the size of my head. I was mixed with African-American and Samoan; he felt my heritage had something to do with it. He really got on my nerves, especially the way he acted when he thought I was getting ready to tell a long story. Whenever I approached him and began to speak, he would respond with "Blah, blah, blah, blah, blah, blah, and blah, blah." There have been many instances I have been fuming mad at him. But, when I cooled off, he was the one I confided in. He had the utmost confidence in me as well, that is why he wanted me to help Katie.

THE 360

Working one-on-one with Katie was more difficult than I anticipated. Eventually, Katie's confusion did not end with the drill movements. When I first met her, she hung out with a young man, and everything appeared innocent. Innocence in my mind meant school boy crushes and secret love notes. Like a winter storm in the midst of a hot summer drought, out of nowhere, she began leaning toward girls for physical affection. On occasions, I found her hugged up in a corner with another girl. It became no surprise for me to see her being tongued by her counterpart. I wrecked my brains trying to figure out why Katie suddenly did a 360.

THE TRAGEDY

Then the day came when Top received a phone call. He was instructed to not let Katie go home from school until an authorized person came to pick her up. He did not share his rationale with me; however, it did not take long before someone showed up to get Katie. After that day, she was missing from school, and I began trying to reach her. I was anxious to talk to her.

Finally, I made contact, and my anxiety was overshadowed when she began to cry; she blurted out, "My mother shot my stepfather in the head. He had raped me on numerous occasions, and now I am pregnant." After hearing her insanely frightening story, I did not know what to say to her. What do you say to someone who is pregnant by her stepfather and whose mother is in jail for shooting him to death? Before this fatal, climatic event took place, I could sense that she was being tortured by some kind of demon. Finally, I understood why Katie's body may have been at school but her mind was on the other side of town.

Who would have suspected anything of that nature was going on? Besides, Katie's stepfather was a soldier and served his country for almost half a decade. The only other thing I knew of him was that he was a short, bald man who wore glasses, and he picked Katie up after school from time to time. I was speechless and sickened when I found out about what he had done to Katie.

I attained a deep empathy for Katie. I considered myself fortunate to have been brought up in a traditional family setting with the guidance of my parents. Many of her hardships were created by the instability of her environment. Unlike her, I was brought up in a traditional and loving family. I was also blessed to have married my high school boyfriend, who had previously joined the United States Army. After graduation, I joined him at his duty station. In the transition, I somehow lost contact with Katie, someone I loved very much in spite of her troubles. As I am stable with my married life, I truly wish the same for Katie. One day, I would like to see her again. Hopefully, I will find her leading a prosperous and happy life. Additionally, I hope we will be able to rekindle our friendship.

As sympathetic as I felt for Katie, I felt more empathetic for Katie's mom. From spending a lot of time with Katie, I thought I knew her mother well. As with any caring mother, she was always concerned about Katie. I used to notice her mannerism. She and Katie had some similar traits and behavior. Physical characteristics included blue eyes and blonde hair. I figured Katie's height must have come from her biological dad. Her mother was short but plump. Much like Katie, I never saw her display violence, not even a hint. Honestly, I could not say what I would be driven to do if the man I married raped and impregnated my child. I am sure I would have been under the utmost level of duress. Any mother would be. All I know is that Katie's mother loved her. Two wrongs do not make a right, but Katie's mother made the ultimate sacrifice to prove how much she loved her daughter. She sacrificed herself by killing someone that may have destroyed her daughter's life forever.

CALVIN KERR, JR.

Tears for My Friend, Katie

With her long, blonde
hair, and light blue
eyes, she was
        so pretty.
She was like a down home
        girl,
lost in New York City.

Throughout our routine,
she never kept in step.
Even with the simple moves,
she had no clue.
She cried out for help.
I tried so hard to be
her
        friend.
I stood by her through
thick and thin.

Several months passed,
She was not in school.
I was afraid she would
        eventually,
fail from the three-day
rule.

When she came back,
she was expecting a
baby.
that's when I cried,
, and I cried, a
river of tears for my
friend Katie.
That's when I cried, and
I cried, a river of
tears for my friend
Katie,
Katie, with the light blue eyes.

It was plain to see her
life
        change in a crude
way.
I remember when she
kissed
        boys back in the
day.
She gravitated to girls,
        for a little while.
She was confused like a
        homeless cat,
that ran wild.
The back and forth,
from boys to girls,
was not the worst secret
in
        her life.
Her baby daddy was
killed,

by her mother who was
his
        wife.

Several months passed,
She was not in school.
I was afraid she would
        eventually,
fail from the three-day
rule.
When she came back,
she was expecting a
baby.
That's when I cried, and I cried, a
river of tears for my
friend, Katie.
That's when I cried, and
I cried, a river of
tears for my friend,

Katie, Katie with the light blue eyes.
It was strictly a case of
another child being,
sexually abused.
Her mother felt she did
what
    she had to do
Now, she is doing her
time in
    a prison cell.
One must wonder if her
man
    punched his ticket,
to go straight to hell.
Maybe she'll get
justice,

and just spend a year or
two. Or, maybe the jury will
    understand the
stress,
she faced from her
child's
    abuse.

Several months passed,
she was not in school.
I was afraid she would
eventually,
fail from the three-day
rule.
When she came back,
she was expecting a
baby.
That's when I cried, ,and I cried, a
river of tears for my
friend, Katie.
That's when I cried, and
I cried, a river of
tears for my friend

Katie, Katie with the light blue eyes..

X-CAPE FROM PANAMA

X-Cape The Environment

Kevin and I used our machetes as we slashed a path through the jungle, literally crawling at times with two of the heaviest weapons any infantryman would have in his arsenal. I carried a 90mm recoilless weapon while Kevin carried an M60 machine, as he was on point leading a company-size element up one of the highest mountains in Panama. It took us more than six hours to conquer it, and every item of clothing on our bodies was soaked. Right in the center of the mountain, in a clearance, stood a small adobe building with enormous spider webs strung from it to the wood line. From that view point, we could see all of Panama City and other outlying towns or villages. While in garrison, on that same day, Federal Marshals from Balboa came to arrest two of our fellow soldiers for possession and distribution of cocaine on a federal installation. Earlier, they were pulled out of formation and forbidden to join us as we embarked upon the mission of climbing the mountain.

Amassed with dense jungles and inhabited by some of the most deadly creatures and vegetation on the face of the earth, Panama City sits on the Pacific Ocean side of the Central American country of Panama. The country boasts numerous islands on both the Atlantic and Pacific oceans. The Canal Zone gives passageway to hundreds of ships a day, providing a shortcut between the two oceans. The zone was governed by the city of Balboa, a territory of the United States government. I can recall the many moments we geared up with our M16s, bullet proof vests, shields, M17s (protective masks), and other equipment for a show of force on its locks.

Otherwise, the isthmus looks calm as seen from above. The safe haven of the aircraft and the view of its beaches can be deceiving. The ambiance of the beaches and ocean waves can at times cast a relaxing spell on the average being; but the mosquitoes, sand fleas, flying ants, scorpions, parasites, and like creatures can make for unpleasant moments. As we ventured into the jungle, one of my comrades would often quip, "These mosquitoes seem to be armed with knives and forks. What's more frightening is that they show up in a convoy of pickup trucks. There is no use in putting on repellent because it gets them high, and they bite and trip off you even more."

Mosquitoes are not the only pests to be cognizant of while conducting operations in the jungle. The diverse inhabitants of the jungle live by the old cliché "it is a dog-eat-dog world." Animals and creatures prowl, hide, camouflage, deceive, and do almost anything to capture its prey or to keep from being preyed upon. To think that avoiding creatures and animals, such as the many classifications of snakes, wild cats, monkeys, bats, and other mutants, would be enough of a hazard, but suddenly, one is reminded of the painful effects of plants as well. The poisonous needles of some (like black palm) and the appetite of others are not very human friendly. Just when you think you have seen it all, the terrain underneath your feet begins to sink. The thick terrain may camouflage a deep waterfall. Land may suddenly give way. Who knows what creatures lurk in caves and caverns, along with the many other dangers, natural or manmade, that they may bear? As a teenager, the thought of facing the aforementioned scenarios never entered my mind. Yet I found myself amidst it all during my tour of duty in the country of Panama.

THE BUDDY PLAN

Upon my entry into the United States Army, I became known as Private (PVT) James Cobbs, better known as Sahee in high school days. My active duty assignment began on 26 August 1971, approximately two months after high school graduation. Knowing my parents barely had enough funds to feed our immediate family, I felt serving my country would be beneficial for me, as well as relieve my parents of another mouth to feed.

I joined the army on the Buddy Plan with a choice of assignment. Personally, I had the opportunity to pursue other options as far as jobs are concerned; however, to be stationed with my friend for the duration of a three-year obligation, we both joined as infantrymen. I know it sounds insane with the Vietnam War going on and soldiers losing their lives every day. It was the guarantee of being stationed together in Panama that sounded intriguing.

My buddy, Kevin Cole, and I were like two book ends, for he was also as dark as chocolate with smooth skin. We both stood about six feet two inches tall. We complemented each other's sense of humor. In high school, we attended most classes together. We drank and attended football games together. Needless to say, we were very close.

Kevin was a bit more athletic than I realized. However, I think we talked about the same amount of BS, although he did get selected as the most loquacious for our senior class. With that little bit of incentive, he was determined to be an asset to the nation one way or another. He wanted to elude the street corners where he witnessed brothers from the neighborhood spending their time begging for nickels and dimes. With their profits, they purchased whiskey, wine, or something to smoke. So, to alleviate me, as well as himself, from that negative environment, he wanted me, his friend, to follow him.

The Buddy Plan took us to basic training at Fort Campbell, Kentucky. The bus ride seemed to take forever and day, possibly because of the anticipation and the mystique of the unknown journey. The first leg of the unknown journey began when we were madly greeted by Drill Sergeant Dale Redding (DS "R"). From the time he stepped on the bus, he became Kevin's personal nightmare. DS R was quick to admit he was an atheist. His attitude and behavior did not dissuade one bit. He had a reddish skin tone, and at six feet four inches tall, he was an imposing figure. His long neck stretched as he stared you down with evil green eyes.

THE HILLBILLY

On many occasions, he caught Kevin in the act of doing something mischievous. One time after lights out, he caught him giving this hillbilly from West Virginia a shower with scouring powder and a scrub brush. Clearly, this time, Kevin did not initiate the incident. I sympathized with Kevin because he had just received an Article 15 for falling asleep on fireguard. For that, he was already pulling extra duty, and he was restricted to the barracks.

This time he was caught red-handed with Ajax in one and a brush in the other. Before that moment, he was awakened by the other privates. They informed Kevin of the surprise shower planned for Private Jonas Williams; however, they did not quite know how to go about it. Out of frustration, Kevin jumped up, went downstairs to the shower, took off all his clothes, and grabbed the Ajax and brush. With no assistance, he began scrubbing PVT Williams. In the climax of it all, guess who appeared? That's right, DS R. The first thing he yelled was, "PVT Cole, get those people in bed. The Officer of the Day (OD) is making his rounds." And sure enough, it was the same OD that accompanied DS R when Kevin had dozed off on fireguard. As soon as Kevin slid under the covers of his bunk, the OD shined the flashlight in Kevin's eyes. Kevin pretended to be asleep. The next morning, it did not take a rocket scientist to figure out he had not gotten a good night's sleep. He worried about the consequences of his actions all night. He anxiously waited to be singled out during the accountability formation before movement to training. It did not happen, and Kevin's worry had to last several more hours. However, it was put to rest when something very peculiar occurred. The hillbilly walked up to him, and in an appreciative tone stated, "I want to thank you for what you did for me last night. My whole body feels nice and clean. Why, I never felt so good in all my life." He reached out, grabbed and shook Kevin's' hands. Kevin stood in with an ambiguous look on his face. He was so shocked; he was unable to respond. Later, he found out that after the senior DS found out about the incident, he suggested the hillbilly thank Kevin for taking interest in his personal hygiene.

After training that day, the interest in the hillbilly's personal hygiene was taken to another level when we ripped PVT William's bunk apart. He had never exchanged his linen since the beginning of basic, almost two months had passed. His sheets, blankets, and mattress accumulated stains and small insect-like creatures. The sight and smell of his bunk area were disgusting to the point of making one want to puke. The entire first floor had to be disinfected and sanitized.

The Ajax affair brought about some lessons learned. One, we learned that PVT Williams grew up in an environment without running water. At home, a bath for him meant a dip in the creek. He knew little about tubs and showers or about water coming from indoor faucets. Two, we learned the meaning of teamwork. The reality that we came from all walks of life created barriers between us that we really were not interested in overcoming. Barriers such as skin color, religion, speech, socialization, customs, and other differences. The display of teamwork while accomplishing the task of a sanitary place to reside had provided us with a mutual understanding for once.

SHOWING OFF

Now all Kevin had to do was gain a mutual understanding with DS R. Although he constantly harassed Kevin, sometimes, Kevin brought attention to himself. Like the time during physical training (PT), the privates had to race each other. It was a fifty-meter race one way and another fifty on the turn around. Kevin had such a big lead against his opponent on the first leg; he would run backward on the second. DS R challenged Kevin and made a bet with him. The bet entailed Kevin being taken off extra duty if he won. He had to do one hundred push-ups if he lost. On the signal to start the race, DS R tripped Kevin. Kevin was so mad that he did not continue. I witnessed the same lowdown trick a bully pulled on him in high school. He ended up fighting the bully and receiving a suspension. I did not think he would punch DS R. Would he? I was relieved when he dropped and did the push-ups despite his anguish.

For some unknown reason, DS R put up with me. Sometimes we talked casually. One day, we were trying to figure out who could jump the highest. Using a pencil, we marked the height of our jump on an old World War II wooden barracks. Here comes Kevin, bragging, "Y'all can't jump." Why did he even go there? DS R took the challenge. Sure enough, Kevin beat us, upsetting DS R; so he pushed Kevin to muscle failure. Muscle failure is when the body will not allow you to physically perform anymore no matter how hard you try.

By the time we were scheduled to take the Army Physical Fitness Readiness Test, Kevin was in topnotch condition thanks to DS R and all the push-ups. He achieved the maximum score on all events. The events included horizontal bars, run dodge and jump, push-ups, sit-ups, the inverted crawl, and one-mile run. Although he maxed out on all events, Kevin was most impressive when he set a record in the inverted crawl event. The event required utilizing hands and feet with the front portion of the body in the upward position. It looked much like a spider. You had to crawl forward on the first leg and backward on the second leg. No one had ever performed it in eleven seconds, but another private in Bravo Company did it in twelve seconds. That set a competition between Kevin and the other Pvt. Hundreds of privates and DSs crowded around the mats to see the action. They were not disappointed. Quickly, Kevin took the lead. He led all the way until he looked back right as he was about to cross the finish line and the other private scooted passed him. Kevin's cockiness got the best of him that time because if he had not taken the time to look back, he would have won.

A Taste Of Failure

I must mention that a few days leading up to the APFRT was one of the few times Kevin had not excelled in one of the requirements of completed basic. He missed Basic Rifle Marksmanship by one target the first time around. The thought of being a failure made him nervous and restless because he knew he would have to be recycled. He did not want to stay a day past our scheduled graduation date; besides, he was also up for his first promotion. He could not wait to get back to the range and get it over with. On the day of the re-fire, it was raining, which presented another obstacle for Kevin. He kept complaining of raindrops clogging his rear sights. Yet an angry and determined Kevin exceeded the standards of marksmanship with a score that normally would qualify for sharpshooter. Sharpshooter was the second highest level after expert.

Fort Puke

A couple of days after BRM, we were promoted and we graduated from basic. We took a bus ride from Fort Campbell to Fort Polk, Louisiana, for Advanced Individual Training (AIT). All we heard about Fort Polk were tales of crocodiles and rice. The hearsay came to be true, for almost every meal, we had rice and every now and then we captured a baby crocodile. One thing people forgot to mention was the weather. It changed as frequently as *Sybil* changed personalities in the movie by the same name. One moment, the sun shined. The next moment, it rained with thunder and lightning. A few minutes later, it snowed. Afterward, the temperature dropped. The cycle was ongoing, but we never stopped training. One day, we set through blistering rain to watch a demonstration of an amphibious vehicle we would never use or see again.

Our stay at Fort Polk was extended by two weeks. Because we took Air Force Junior Reserve Officer Training in high school, we were selected to attend the leadership preparation course prior to our actual AIT. The course had very strict requirements. Demerits (gigs) were given for a single wrinkle in your blanket. Boots had to be spit-shined. Mustaches were measured, and every strand of hair had to be in place. Military bearing had to be upheld at all time. In other words, we had to be "spit and polish" in every respect. That course would later benefit us as we would be promoted to corporal after four weeks of being on active duty in Panama.

The Lock Up

Fort Polk was the first place that Kevin ever saw the inside of a jail cell. Specifically, the jail was located in a small backwoods town right outside Fort Polk. Its name was Leesville. We nicknamed it Diseaseville. The jailing occurred on a weekend pass. We had to pick a battle buddy in order to go to town. For various reasons, Kevin could not afford to get in trouble, so he chose PVT William Lawrence as his battle buddy. PVT Lawrence was from Boston, Massachusetts. He was about five feet ten inches tall, and a big-boned brother with a mustache. He was the quiet type, and that is why Kevin selected him. Kevin had no idea that his evening was about to take a wild turn. We started out together. The town did not have many clothing stores. We found one with some pants that we liked. Brother Emmitt "Red" Douglas from Detroit provided me a lesson on shoplifting. The trick was to take a few pair of pants to the dressing room while the clerk was making a sale. Once in the dressing room, we slipped a new pair of pants on under our old pants.

After shopping, we split up and decided to meet back up at the"Red Rooster", a club that we heard rumors about from people on post. The club was known for pimps and prostitutes. Before they entered the club, Kevin and William followed a prostitute into a tattoo shop. William said a few words to her while Kevin just smiled. Then they decided to walk next door to the club. Kevin ordered a beer and William ordered a whiskey sour. Almost instantaneously, after William drank his whiskey sour, his behavior changed. He started cursing the waitress, so Kevin took him outside. Kevin never figured that taking him outside would escalate the situation. Why did he do that? The same prostitute they met in the tattoo shop was the first person William saw. He went after her. He muttered, "Come here you B and give me some of that P." He began to manhandle her. She tried to get away by going back into the tattoo shop, but William followed her in there. He grabbed and pulled on her until she slapped him. He Jap-slapped her back, and she ran out of the shop for help. Kevin decided to wave for a taxi. Momentarily, the taxi driver stopped; but before Kevin could get William in the taxi, the driver pulled off. Now they were surrounded by prostitutes and the pimps. The 5-0 had never been such a welcomed sight. The officer got the details and took Kevin and William to jail. He left both of them in a cell for a while. Finally, he took a statement from Kevin and gave him a ride back to the barracks.

The next morning, the first sergeant (1SG) had Kevin in his office for a long time, standing at parade rest. He told the first sergeant the same story he related to me and the arresting police officer. He reiterated the fact that he had a beer and William had a whiskey sour. Kevin suggested, "I think someone slipped a Mickey in his drink." That same day, William was placed back in military custody. He was given extrajudicial punishment; basically, it consisted of extra duty and restriction. No civil charges were filed. That incident seemed to alert all the drill sergeants to keep a close eye on Kevin. He often asked me, "I wonder why I am the first person questioned when something goes down in and around the barracks. If someone gets into a fight, they ask me about it. They found a homemade bomb under the barracks the other day; what the hell do I know about making a bomb? What is it? Do I have the look of an instigator or what? Don't they know that I am just a naïve country boy from Memphis, Tennessee? I don't know anything."

DUTY IN PANAMA

Needless to say, Kevin was glad to see graduation day. We went home for a few days and then took a flight out of Charleston, South Carolina, to Panama City, Panama. As the plane hovered over Panama, I could see the dense jungle, white sand, and numerous islands. The heat smacked us right dab in the face as we made our departure from the plane to the air force base terminal. We secured our bags and someone from Headquarters Company greeted us and took us to Fort Kobbe for in-processing. The personnel at Headquarters Company assigned us to Bravo Company.

While assigned to Bravo Company, Kevin and I were responsible for two of the heaviest hand-carried weapons in the army. I carried the 90 mm. It was like a bazooka. Kevin carried the M60 machine gun. It was not as heavy as the 90 mm but it came with an extra barrel and tripod. Additionally, we had to carry our rounds. Carrying those weapons was no joke. The experience was worse when you had to cut through thick jungle and carry all food and clothing for a couple of weeks. Many times Kevin was on point as well.

The barracks were welcomed sites as we returned from the jungle. However, on one occasion, in a rapid attempt to get back to the pleasant environment of the barracks, one of our comrades went flying around a sharp curbed when his 1/4 ton vehicle flipped. He did not survive the accident. We were often warned of the ease in which one could turn those light vehicles over. Sylvester James did not heed that warning. He was a quiet, short, heavyset brother from the small town of Hopkinsville, Kentucky. He slept next to me and Kevin. I regret that I used to complain about the way he smelt. He would very seldom take a shower after spending weeks in the jungle. He was gone now, and I saw him for the last time at his funeral. It was my first military funeral, and it would not be my last. With the potential of lives being lost and spending time so much time together, everyone pretty much bonded. Our company was notorious for taking pride in everything we were required to do.

We ensured all companies within the battalion heard us when we sounded off with our motto and ended it with "Banditos!" Bravo Company was a straight-leg infantry company with a vast amount of esprit de corps. We were known as the Banditos. We were envied by the other companies because we were very tight-knit and very athletic. We worked hard and we partied hard. People were afraid to walk on our grass or cross one of us. Sometimes, we would come out of the jungle, play a game and return. We won league championships in flag football and basketball.

Although we never won championships in softball, we played it as well. Usually, we intimidated our opponents before the game began.

Flag football was a big event in Panama. Rival teams from local military installations throughout Panama came to play us on our turf and were embarrassed from the whipping we put on them. We ran up high scores like 84 to 6 or 76 to 0. Only one team from Fort Clayton seemed to have our number. Fort Clayton was another United States Army installation on the Pacific Oceanside. It was the home of a Mechanized Infantry Battalion we called the Mech.

One of my more memorable games was against the Mech. I played corner while Kevin played free safety. As the captain for the secondary, Kevin would bark out assignments for pass coverage. I had never seen Kevin make many mistakes. When the quarterback threw anywhere in his area, it usually ended up in an interception with a possible runback for a touchdown. Yet, the Mech had a strong-armed quarterback who played a little bit of college ball. They also had a six feet nine wide receiver with college experience as well. As fast as Kevin was, normally, he could eyeball the quarterback and still have the speed to recover for an interception. But this quarterback was deceptive. His strong arm complemented his deception. The height of the wide receiver allowed him to throw the ball higher as well. All these factors led to a score in the end zone over Kevin's head. With that play, the Mech won the game. Later, the Mech players and ours met at the club on Albrook Air Force Base. We discussed the game. They admitted that they probably were more afraid of us than we were of them. Again, the reputation of the Banditos preceded us.

THE BREAK UP

As the months passed we became seasoned soldiers, and we became more familiar with the Panamanian civilians, particularly the females. Moreover, Kevin's Panamanian girlfriend became pregnant with his daughter. He had not given up on his high school sweetheart back in Memphis. He decided to go home and discuss the matter with her. Specifically, he wanted to realize the degree of love and affection she had for him. It was very obvious that Kevin's love for Benita Law was unconditional. Benita was a lovely girl with a tall, slim body frame. She sported a light skin tone with freckles.

Kevin was so determined to see her, particularly after receiving a derogatory letter about her from a classmate. While on leave, he traveled from Memphis to Nashville. Benita was attending Tennessee State University there. He booked a room at a nearby motel and contacted her. When they met, it did not turn out the way Kevin envisioned. He made a mistake by not using tact in questioning her about the behavior described in the letter he received. She tried to explain to him that nothing such as that ever took place. She felt a great deal of mistrust from Kevin, so an argument pursued. Kevin decided to leave the hotel room. He told her, "When I walk out of this room, it will be the last time you will see me. I am not coming back." Little did either of them know that they would not see each other again for thirty-eight years. Only then did they realize that outsiders and domestic pressures had influenced their breakup.

CITY SLICKERS

When we returned to Panama, our lives began to change. *City Slickers* began to show up. They were very influential. Guys like James Coleman from New York, David Thompson from New Orleans, and Dennis Chesley from Chicago saw a chance for profit through drug distribution. We knew very little about marijuana, cocaine, PCP, angel dust, Thai sticks, and other drugs and medication that got you high. Most of the marijuana from Panama was called Panama red. At the time, Kevin and I thought we were cool smoking Kool cigarettes. Almost everyone smoked and drank something. Everything was so inexpensive. For instance, cigarettes were about seventeen cents a pack. A bottle of wine was as little as sixty-eight cents. Fifths of liquor was less than two dollars. Therefore, through the black market, profit could be made on items bought on post as well.

Yet the city slickers focused more on cocaine and marijuana. Those two drugs were easily acquirable during the '70s, especially in Panama. Neighboring countries like Columbia and Peru helped contribute to its availability. The inexpensiveness and the availability certainly lured the city slickers. Soon as they hit the ground, they began buying for use and profit, particularly the rock cocaine, which they cut and sold, almost doubling or tripling their profits. Kevin and I did not know one thing about cutting cocaine (coke) or distributing it. But the city slickers were very capable of those two chores. It bothered me to be around it.

I had a frightening opportunity to see firsthand the largest amount of rock cocaine I ever saw or will ever see. My Panamanian friend, Felix, was someone I met through my Panamanian girlfriend. Felix and I became close so he took me into his confidence and wanted to show me something. He knew the locations of places the Guardia Nacional, Panama's largest law enforcement agency, bagged cocaine. He took me there. When I entered the house with police, strapped with grease guns and "oozies" (Uzi) everywhere, I was so scared that I almost pissed on myself. All the heavily armed policemen and the crystallized rock cocaine set out on the tables overwhelmed me. I did not dare let on that I was an American soldier. I kept wondering why I let myself be put in such a life threatening position. I saw millions of dollars' worth of crystal cocaine along with huge amounts of money and various types of weapons. Finally, I was highly relieved when we got out of there alive. When I was long gone from Panama, I found out that Felix was murdered by the Guardia Nacional.

In the meantime, while I was still there, the city slickers were well at work. They were unaware that the Canal Zone law enforcement along with the criminal investigative detectives (CID) on post had started to move in. Dennis Chesley was the first to be arrested. He and Thompson had formed an alliance. The cocaine was the only mutually exclusive thing that brought them together.

Chesley grew up on the south side of Chicago. He was a short, hairy Caucasian with African-American traits. Although he was scrawny, he was very courageous. Once, he scuffled with a big, burly Military Police officer (MP) and survived the altercation without a scratch. When I saw the MP, it was funny to see his swollen face and puffy black eyes. He had attempted to apprehend Chesley for smoking a joint (a cigarette made of marijuana). Actually, Chesley called it a roach (less than half of a joint). Anyway, the MP needed backup because he never would have apprehended Chesley alone. Eventually, he received assistance from some of his fellow officers. Chesley told us the story after his release back to Bravo Company.

THE FELONIES

After that incident, he made the mistake of selling less than an ounce of coke to a CID agent. On that very night, Chesley informed me that he was about to make a deal. Curiously, I followed him into the company's club. He met with a plain-clothed, short Caucasian guy, and together, they entered the latrine. One of the stalls was used to pass the coke and money. The next day, authorities apprehended Chesley and locked him up in a Balboa cell.

Kevin and I showed up for Chesley's trial to testify that he was with us in the barracks when the sale took place. We were warned by fellow soldiers that testifying may bring suspicion on us. We had to do what we could to keep a fellow soldier from going to jail. Because it happened on post, he was being charged with a felony and not a misdemeanor. Despite our attempts to help him, he was found guilty. I believe Chesley squealed on Thompson because Thompson never came to see him while in jail nor did he show up at the trial. Thompson fronted the money for Chesley to buy the coke. I could tell Chesley was disappointed with Thompson from his expressions during our visits.

The next one to be apprehended was James Coleman (J.C.), a tall, black, dapper brother from New York. He was so cool and stylish with his dress. He appeared to have all the answers, especially when it came to purchasing and distributing cocaine. Within months of his arrival, he found suppliers. J.C. began to make a lot of loot. He wore fancy suits and outfits that he could afford to have customized in downtown Panama. His jewelry was personalized, usually bearing his name. His gold bracelets and necklaces were embedded with precious stones. He fashioned diamond rings and earrings. He was on top of the world. And then one day, right before we left for the jungle, he was arrested right in front of the formation. Law officials from the District Attorney's office in Balboa read him his rights. It was perhaps one of J.C. most embarrassing moments. I was stunned. I could not help but think that I could have been trapped in that same situation. My envy could have been my demise. His fancy clothes and rolls of money did not matter now. The most valuable thing that matters in life (freedom) had been taken away from J.C.

THE ESCAPE

Somehow, J.C. made bail. Obviously, the money from his mom, relatives, and friends played its part to suffice the required amount of bail money. But I was puzzled that he was actually released to our company commander and no one had to watch him. J.C. took full advantage of that. He began to plan his escape route. When he spoke, he was on pins and needles. He trusted Kevin and me so much that he uncovered his entire plan to us. As he spoke, he was folding clothes and stuffing toilet items in his bag. The only thing he did not tell us was the when. The when came the very next morning. He was absent without leave (AWOL). He had taken flight while Dennis Chesley was locked away somewhere in a federal penitentiary. We never knew what happened to J.C. We thought of many unanswered questions: Did he succeed? Was he a casualty of the hostile territory he traveled during his escape? Did he take refuge in another country? James Coleman was never seen nor heard in Panama again since that night we witnessed him pack his bags to escape.